RUSSIA'S SECURITY AND
THE WAR ON TERROR

This book discusses and provides examples of Russia's need to reshape its security and military policies in order to meet the global challenges of fighting terrorism and counterinsurgency. It addresses some of the problems facing Russia's national security and military power, including:

- Military reform
- US-Russian relations
- The political economy of Russian security policy
- Russian policy regarding the proliferation of weapons of mass destruction
- The chances for US-Russian cooperation in ballistic missile defence

Russia's Security and the War on Terror provides an insight into Russian military policies and its changing relationship with NATO throughout the 1990s.

This book was previously published as a special issue of *The Journal of Slavic Military Studies*.

Mikhail Tsypkin is an Associate Professor of national security at the Naval Postgraduate School in Monterey, USA.

RUSSIA'S SECURITY AND THE WAR ON TERROR

edited by Mikhail Tsypkin

Routledge
Taylor & Francis Group

LONDON AND NEW YORK

First published 2008
by Routledge
2 Park Square, Milton Park, Abingdon, Oxfordshire OX14 4RN

Simultaneously published in the USA and Canada
by Routledge
711 Third Avenue, New York, NY 10017

First issued in paperback 2014

*Routledge is an imprint of the Taylor & Francis Group,
an informa business*

© 2008 Edited by Mikhail Tsypkin

Typeset in Times by RefineCatch Ltd, Bungay, Suffolk

British Library Cataloguing in Publication Data
A catalogue record for this book is available from the British Library

Library of Congress Cataloging in Publication Data
A catalog record has been requested

ISBN 13: 978-1-138-87371-1 (pbk)
ISBN 13: 978-0-415-39055-2 (hbk)

CONTENTS

Introduction

MIKHAIL TSYPKIN[1]

Russian military is not well prepared to meet the challenges of fighting terrorism and counterinsurgency. President Vladimir Putin has spoken repeatedly about the need to reshape the Russian military to confront the new tasks, but relatively little progress has been achieved. Resistance of the military's corporate self-interest is an important obstacle to change: the top brass prefer to maintain a hollow military designed for fighting a global war, to serious restructuring and downsizing (including a transition to an all-volunteer force) that would result in a reduction of the number of billets for seniors officers. The military can persist in their attachment to the Cold War posture because the politicians have failed to provide for Russia's security by building an alliance with NATO.

Russian politics have been in flux for more than a decade, and so have Russian security and military policies. Since 1991, Russian national security policy has veered from anticipation of equal partnership with the United States (US) in the early 1990s, to the verge of a shooting war with NATO in Kosovo in 1999, to the 'strategic partnership' with the US in the aftermath of the September 11, 2001 terrorist attacks. The armed forces withdrew from Central Europe, survived a collapse of their budget, reduced their size and have redefined their missions and organization structure in Chechnya (1994–96 and 1999 until the present) have presented the Russian military with the challenge of adjusting to counterinsurgency operations. Since 1999, the Russians have described their war against insurgents in Chechnya as a fight against terrorism, a fight in which the Russian military have not been highly successful.

The papers published in this volume were presented at a conference sponsored by the Naval Postgraduate School Foundation and Foreign Military Studies Office of the Department of the Army in Monterey, in September 2003. They address some basic problems facing Russia's national security and military power today: military reform, US-Russian relations, the political economy of Russian security policy, Russian policy regarding the proliferation of weapons of mass destruction (WMD), and the chances for US-Russian cooperation in ballistic missile defense.

After ten years of debate on the subject, is the Russian military establishment finally reforming or not? Aleksandr Golts argues that the Russian high command has avoided real reform. Structural changes have been inconsistent. The goal of a transition to an all-volunteer force has been abandoned in favor of one mixing enlisted conscripts and volunteers (contract soldiers). No serious thought has been given to creating a professional cadre of non-commissioned officers (NCOs). The officer corps continues to suffer from poverty and insufficient professionalism, as well as from a very narrow and outmoded system of education and training. Despite much talk about the military's role in the war against terrorism, the high command is quite reluctant to abandon the mission of fighting NATO.

Two weeks after the papers printed here had been delivered, President Vladimir Putin and Defense Minister Sergei Ivanov unveiled a document entitled *The Current Tasks of Development of the Armed Forces* on 2 October 2003 at a conference in front of the Russian top brass and members of parliament.[2] *The Current Tasks*, as well the remarks by Putin and Ivanov, and some subsequent comments by high-ranking officers, provide a picture generally consistent with Golts' pessimism about the current condition of the Russian military. The term 'military reform' has become so discredited that Putin apparently has decided to get rid of it: military reform, he proclaimed, consisted of cutting personnel and reducing redundancy in the organization of the armed forces, both processes quite unpopular with the officer corps. He insisted that the period of 'radical reform' of the military was over, and that a period of 'profound transformation' which will result in 'qualitatively' different armed forces was beginning.[3] The time had come, said Putin, to change the military manpower system, to equip the armed forces with new weapons and create a new mobilization system adequate to new threats.

The Currents Tasks, a lengthy document (73 pages), provides ample and frank evidence of the problems that have to be fixed. No progress has been made in reducing dependence on conscripts, while the size of the draft pool is declining precipitously; all attempts to raise the standard of living of officers have failed; the system of military education is in disarray and outdated; the weapons are rapidly becoming obsolete.

What about the future? The most painful issue, that of moving from the draft to a volunteer force (the Russian term is *kontraktniki* – 'contract soldiers'), is to be resolved by mixing the two approaches. The quantitative parameters of this transition presented by Golts, have been confirmed in *The Current Tasks*. It appears that under the best circumstances not more than one quarter of the enlisted personnel (147,5000) will become 'contract soldiers' by the end of 2007.[4] Even this rather modest plan must have caused considerable unease among the officer corps, or at least among the high command, judging by the cautious language in which the future transition has been described:

The partial transition of the Armed Forces to the contract basis is not the goal of their development and improvement, but the means to strengthen defenses of the Russian Federation and increase combat ability of the Armed Forces. The decision to transfer some of the units to the contract basis is not a political declaration, unsubstantiated financially and organizationally, but is the result of a lengthy process of evaluation of the objective capabilities of the country.[5]

The authors of *The Current Tasks* found it necessary to say that the government's commitment to the partially 'contract' forces was *not* a political gesture, probably because the issue of military draft is so political in Russia: conscription is so unpopular that President Yeltsin, desperately fighting for re-election in 1996, had to promise to end conscription, a pledge that has never been kept. Apparently, Putin is putting pressure on the officer corps to accept the coming change: they should believe both that the president means business, and that the unwelcome novelty is dictated by the needs of the military, who are facing a 'demographic pit' – a sharp decline of the draft pool in 2005–10.[6] Still, politics appear to be an important consideration for Putin, who, as noted, is up for re-election in 2004. 'Contract soldiers' are supposed to replace conscripts first of all in the theater of war in Chechnya,[7] which holds out a promise to Russia's parents that their children will not have to fight in that war.

The draft, therefore, will not be eliminated. Just as Golts predicted, it will continue to provide the majority of enlisted personnel in the military, border guards and internal troops, and to ensure that the armed forces have a mobilization reserve.[8] Why? The official explanation is that, in addition to the expense of an all-volunteer military, it will be unable to produce enough reservists for mobilization. The reserves are to be mobilized if the 'permanently ready' forces based on 'contract soldiers' fail to deter or localize a military conflict that Russia is involved in.[9] Golts explains the behavior of the Russian top brass by their self-interest: as long as the armed forces are based on a system of mass mobilization, the high command can preserve an excessive number of billets for senior officers (justified by the requirement to fill positions in new divisions mobilized for war), exercise control over considerable industrial mobilization capacities and avoid dealing with the post-superpower realities of Russian security policies.

A contradictory threat assessment appears to be behind this vision of a mixed volunteer/conscript military. On the one hand, *The Current Tasks* states that the military danger to Russia is 'relatively low', and that none of today's military conflicts 'directly threatens Russia's security'.[10] Among the major directions of Russia's security policy are increasing interoperability of the Russian military with the forces of NATO members, and strengthening 'strategic partnership' with the US, especially within the framework of the coalition against terror (which *The Current Tasks* refer to as 'an element of global stability and a means for establishing a more just world order').[11] The document in effect recognizes that the US military presence in Central Asia is in Russia's interest: 'destabilization in Afghanistan' and return of the threat of 'Islamic extremism' in that theater (read: US withdrawal from Central Asia) would increase the military burden for Russia.[12]

In a sharp break with the Soviet tradition of threat assessment, which regarded the liberal democratic countries of the West as just as threatening as Nazi Germany, *The Current Tasks* recognizes that it is the liberal democratic character of the most powerful Western nations, with its transparency and predictability, that makes Russia safe – and that weakening of liberal democracies in the West would be a threat to Russia.[13]

On the other hand, *The Current Tasks* continues to refer to the danger from 'military alliances' growing at the expense of Russia's security (read: NATO enlargement).[14] Furthermore, the document refers to NATO's allegedly 'offensive military doctrine' as a threat to Russia.[15] The American R&D work on low-yield nuclear weapons is also described as a threat, albeit an indirect one: it may encourage nuclear proliferation and lower the threshold of nuclear weapons use, thus destabilizing the international situation.[16] Thus, even though it is recognized that the level of immediate military threat has declined, Russia finds itself unable to exclude any kind of military threat: from her southern neighbors, from China (this threat goes unmentioned, but is not explicitly dismissed either) and from her 'strategic partners', NATO and the US.

This worldview of the Russian political-military leadership also means that Russia does not have reliable and strong allies with whom it could divide the labor of its military effort. Therefore, Russia has to rely very much on mobilizing its own resources, including manpower. The Russian generals have put the plank quite low when it comes to reliance on their standing military: the 'permanently ready' forces, manned by a mixture of 'contract soldiers' and conscripts, should be able to fight two simultaneous local conflicts, and to provide for strategic deployment and mobilization of the armed forces in a larger conflict.[17] Even though *The Current Tasks* says that the size of the mobilization reserve should be reduced, the document holds out no hope of getting rid of the draft, which provides the bulk of trained reservists.[18]

Is there a chance that Russia would move to volunteer reserves, following the American model? This is not very likely. It appears that Russian officers genuinely cannot imagine armed forces that do not rely on conscription for mobilizing reserves. Thus, First Deputy Chief of General Staff Colonel General Yuri Baluevsky (whom Golts described as 'one of the smartest and most non-conformist of Russian generals') recently said that the Americans:

...have completely preserved the draft system, and today are forming three brigades out of conscript reservists in order to send them to Iraq.[19]

The American experience in Iraq may yet provide a further argument in favor of retaining the draft. The limitations on the American mission by relatively small size of reserves will in all likelihood be noticed by the Russian military, who could make an argument that a small all-volunteer military does a good job winning a local conflict, but simply does not have the numbers for cementing political victory by putting enough boots on the ground. The outcomes of the US campaigns in Iraq and Afghanistan are likely to affect the future of Russian military reform, in as far as the reformers in Russia, who advocate all-volunteer, relatively small, highly mobile military have been inspired by the American successes in the Persian Gulf war of 1991, Kosovo in 1999, Afghanistan in 2001 and in the destruction of the Iraqi military in 2003. If the US finds, as Andrew Krepinevich suggests, a strategy that would allow an effective employment of a force that can be realistically sustained,[20] the position of military reformers in Russia will be strengthened. If the US fails, the voices of those arguing in favor of a military ready for a mass mobilization of conscripts, will become louder.

The difficulty that Russia has in building reliable alliances that might alleviate the need to have a large mobilization system is well demonstrated by Aleksandr Belkin in his paper on US-Russian relations. He points to the narrow overlap of the two nations' security interests. Both agree about the danger of Islamic fundamentalism; Bush noted their mutual concern about this issue after his first meeting with Putin in June 2001.[21] Cooperation in the war on terror has improved US-Russian relations, but, as Belkin observes:

> ... the new US-Russian rapprochement rests on a very delicate basis: the personal relationship of the two national leaders. While it is very important for a genuine trust and better understanding, it cannot be sufficient for building a stable structure of bilateral relations. The Putin-Bush interaction cannot substitute for the US-Russian relations. In this case President Reagan's formula that 'It takes two to tango' should be read as a concert of nations, of political and business elites, not only of leading individuals.

There are, however, differences even in this area: Putin sees the center of gravity for the war on terror in Saudi Arabia and Pakistan, while Bush has put emphasis on Iraq.[22] The ambiguous nature of US-Russian relations was stressed by the Minister of Defense, Sergei Ivanov, who said in October 2003 that, although the relations between the two nations had improved since the days of the Cold War, and they are no longer enemies, they were 'definitely' not allies.[23] US ambassador to Russia Alexander Vershbow agreed with Ivanov, adding that '[t]he US-Russian partnership covers a broad range of subjects, but we have not reached the point where we consider ourselves part of the same family – in contrast with the relationships that the United States has with its traditional allies in Europe and Asia'.[24] This view very much agrees with Belkin's.

The predictable American response to problems in relations with other nations is to suggest that they become more democratic – according to this logic, the more the public can influence foreign policy, the better it will be for the given nation's relations with the US. Belkin, however, makes a very different suggestion: the Russian leaders should ignore public opinion when making foreign policy decisions, since the Russian public tends to react too emotionally to world events. Indeed, the outraged reaction of the Russian public to NATO's campaign in Kosovo, various anti-American actions by the Duma (the lower house of the parliament) and consistently negative views of the US found in surveys of Russian public opinion, suggest that a foreign policy directly reflecting popular preferences would hardly improve US-Russian relations.

Mikhail Pogorely notes in his paper on US-Russian cooperation in non-proliferation of WMD that this cooperation is difficult and US-Russian perspectives on this issue are quite different. The Russian side frequently suspects that the American efforts to secure nuclear materials in Russia are part of a plan to unilaterally disarm Russia. Despite the shared desire to prevent proliferation of WMD, US efforts against proliferation of nuclear capabilities are often seen in Russia as a desire to drive Russia out of nuclear energy markets. Pogorely suggests that the lack of a clear 'political strategy' leaves the public confused about, if not hostile to, the West. Every US-Russian cooperative endeavor requires, as Alexsander Savelyev points out addressing the issue of ballistic missile defense, a 'stable US-Russian relationship', which, in its own turn, requires 'the success of democratic reforms in Russia, effectiveness of the struggle against international terrorism, the results of military reform in Russia and many other things'. Unfortunately, Russia's progress towards all of these objectives remains uncertain.

Russia's geopolitical isolation may gradually become a consciously chosen policy. Vitaly Shlykov, in his paper on Putin's attack against Russia's most powerful businessmen – the 'oligarchs' – notes the change that has taken place in the government during Putin's three years in office:

... the elite has become more militarized and less intellectual. Whereas in the early 1990s the elite's strategic core consisted mainly of economists, under Putin military men and security officers have gained the upper hand in shaping national strategy. This has altered the state's priorities with issues of security, military reform and the country's geopolitical place in the world coming very much to the fore.

This new elite hopes to strengthen the government's control over extraction of natural resources and increase taxation of such businesses, thus replenishing the treasury. Indeed, in an interview in November 2003, Defense Minister Ivanov said that 'mineral and energy resources belong to the state, they are not private property'.[25] Shlykov suggests that such a shift in economic policy might directly benefit Russia's defense industry: this money could be used to revive the defense industry, and produce a trickle-down effect helping to propel Russia into the era of high technology. Shlykov notes that some prominent Russian economists have been promoting such ideas.

Whatever the real chances of such plans, they are likely to contribute to Russia's isolation on the world scene.

First, a buildup of the defense industry does require certain political justification. Keeping Russia estranged from the West will allow the government to justify increased defense spending.

Second, a pursuit of such a plan may make its authors hope that Russia could preserve the autarkic nature of its defense industry, thus saving them from the need to cooperate in weapons production with other nations. If such cooperation is not necessary, Russia has one more reason to do without alliances with strong partners.

We are facing a situation quite typical of Russian politics today: Putin charts a course meant to bring Russia more closely to the West, while some of his actions may bring about the opposite results. In the 1990s, Western observers justifiably complained that the weakened and dysfunctional Russian state prevented Russia's progress towards market economy and democratic political system, and therefore her better integration with the West.[26] As if in response, Putin is working to strengthen the state. This state, however, is based on the remnants of Soviet bureaucracy, with its organizational culture intact, thanks to the revolution from above which spared whole state structures complete with their employees. The security services and the military were the bulwark of the Soviet state and they, unlike the communist party, were spared (although downsized) during the collapse of the Soviet system. Thus, the return of the state means the return of the Soviet mindset, albeit considerably attenuated, as noted by Shlykov, by years of living without communism. The role of the so-called *siloviki* – personalities from the 'power agencies' (*silovye structury*) – has been additionally enhanced by the fact that Russia has been at war (although an undeclared one) in Chechnya since 1999.

In the view of the *siloviki* Russia can be only the central and dominant element of any alliance that Moscow takes part in. In the Soviet past, there is no experience of playing the role of a junior partner; even an alliance of near-equals turned out to be elusive in the case of Sino-Soviet relations. Finding a place in the international security system commensurate with Russia's reduced economic and military resources is not easy for the *siloviki*. They have been very uncomfortable about Putin's decision to share the burden of fighting Islamism by going along with the US military presence in Central Asia.

One should note, for the sake of fairness, that it is not easy for Russia to find an alliance that is both not dominated by her and still serves her security needs. Because of Russia's immense size and presence in different geopolitical regions, these needs can be met only with considerable difficulty. How willing, for instance, would NATO be to guarantee Russia's security vis-à-vis China? And wouldn't such a guarantee, if obtained, not sour Russia's relations with her great eastern neighbor? Still, Russia tends to make things more difficult for herself by exaggerating threats, especially those allegedly presented on its western periphery by NATO. *The Current Tasks*, for instance, assigns Russia's western group of forces, facing Ukraine, Belarus, the Baltic States, Finland and Scandinavia, the mission of 'deterring a large-scale war'.[27] One may doubt that the Russian political and military leadership worry about a real threat of war against NATO. Soon after the publication of *The Current Tasks*, General Baluevsky, the First Deputy Chief of General Staff, was asked about the likelihood of a war against NATO; he responded that while this possibility cannot be 'completely ruled out', such a war would be 'like death for Russia'.[28] Still, the Western direction is present in Russian military plans and uses up scarce resources.

Russia faces today a predicament similar to the one it confronted in the late nineteenth/early twentieth century: Russia saw threats all along its periphery, while Russia's size (which protected it from conquest) and lack of communications made it difficult for troops in one theater to reinforce another one. Therefore, Russia had 'to maintain an enormous permanent armed force that would be capable of defeating all or most its principal enemies simultaneously'.[29] The good news today is that the threat of a major war involving Russia is incomparably lower than it was a century ago. The bad news is that Russia, unlike its tsarist predecessor aligned with France and England, does not have any powerful allies. As a result, the Russian military is 'approximately' one million strong, and will not become smaller.[30] For comparison, active duty armed forces of the US (excluding the Coast Guard), a superpower with global responsibilities, are 1,427,000 strong.[31]

The immediate result of the contradictory political context of military policy is that, four years since Vladimir Putin began his political ascent with proclaiming a 'war on terrorism' in Chechnya, the Russian military has not been reshaped to fight such wars. Chechnya continues to claim the lives of Russian soldiers, while the military now implies that defeating insurgency is not really its job. In the words of General Baluevsky, the armed forces 'did their job' in Chechnya: they 'destroyed and dispersed the formations of the bandits' there.[32] Apparently, constant ambushes of the Russian forces, truck bombs and assassinations are not something the military can handle. It remains to be seen if a military effective in what the pundits refer to as the wars of the twenty-first century can be built in Russia in the near future.

NOTES

1. The views expressed here are those of the author solely, and are not meant to represent the views of the Department of the Navy or any other agency of the US Government.
2. *Aktualnye zadachi razvitiya Vooruzhennikh Sil RF*, <www.mil.ru/index.php? menu_id=886>.
3. Vladimir Putin, *Vstupitel'noe slovo na soveshchanii s rukovodyashchim sostavom Vooruzhennykh Sil Rossii*, 2 Oct. 2003, <www.kremlin.ru>.
4. *Aktualnye zadachi* (note 2) p.54; Vladimir Yevseyev, 'Blagie pozhelaniya I surovaya real'nost'', *Nezavisimoe Voennoye obozrenie*, 11 Nov. 2003, <http://nvo.ng.ru/wars/2003-11–21/1_reality.html>.
5. *Aktualnye zadachi* (note 2) p.49.
6. Ibid. p.51.
7. Ibid. p.54.
8. Ibid. p.55.
9. Ibid. p.53.
10. Ibid. pp.22, 23.
11. Ibid. pp.12, 18.
12. Ibid. p.24.
13. Ibid. p.23.
14. Ibid. p.21.
15. Ibid. p.18.
16. Ibid. p.24.
17. Ibid. p.41.
18. Ibid. p.55.

19. 'Belaya kniga ministerstva oborony', *Rossiyskaya gazeta*, 31 Oct. 2003, <http://rg.ru/2003/10/31/doktrina.html>.

20. Andrew Krepinevich, 'Strategy, Anyone?', *Defense News*, 1 Dec. 2003, p.43.

21. Peggy Noonan, 'A Chat in the Oval Office', *The Wall Street Journal*, 25 June 2001.

22. *Press-konferentsiya Prezidenta V. V. Putina I Prezidenta Dzh. Busha posle rossiysko-amerikanskikh peregovorov*, 22 Nov. 2002, <www.president. kremlin.ru>.

23. Yuliya Kalinina, 'Agent natsional'noi bezopasnosti', *Moskovskiy komsomolets*, 27 Oct. 2003.

24. Alexander Vershbow, *The U.S.-Russia Relationship, Past and Future*, remarks at Moscow State Diplomatic Academy, 18 Nov. 2003, <www.usembassy.ru>.

25. 'Russian Defense Minister Calls for Greater State Control Over Oil Resources', AFP, 17 Nov. 2003.

26. See, for instance, Stephen Holmes, 'What Russia Teaches Us Now', *The American Prospect*, Vol. 8, No. 33, 1 July–1 Aug. 1997, <www.prospect.org/print/V8/33/holmes-s.html>.

27. *Aktualnye zadachi* (note 2) p.47,

28. Aleksandr Babakin *et al.*, 'Belaya kniga ministra oborony', *Rossiyskaya gazeta*, 8 Nov. 2003, <http://rg.ru/2003/10/31/doktrina.html>.

29. Frederick W. Kagan and Robin Higham, 'Introduction', in Frederick W. Kagan and Robin Higham (eds.), *The Military History of Tsarist Russia* (NY: Palgrave 2002) p.3.

30. *Vystuplenie Sergeya Ivanova na soveshchanii v ministerstve oborony RF*, <www.rian.ru/rian/intro.cfm?doc_id=276>.

31. *The Military Balance 2003–2004*, 102/1, p.18.

32. Babakin *et al.* (note 28).

US-Russian Relations and the Global Counter-Terrorist Campaign

ALEXANDER A. BELKIN

With the election of George W. Bush in 2000, the Kremlin had its reservations about the newly elected US president and his administration. For a time, mutual criticism between the two countries seemed to be the rule of the day. Among other things, the US pulled out of the 1972 ABM treaty unilaterally, and Russia prosecuted its war against the Chechen separatists. Then came 9/11, and the two countries found solid ground for mutually advantageous cooperation – the global war on terrorism. But with NATO/Yugoslavia still clearly in the rear-view mirror, and the war against Iraq still ahead, the course of future relations remained unclear. The author examines US-Russian relations as they evolved before and after the war in Iraq and offers conclusions and lessons learned for both sides.

> Russia is an important partner in the war on terror and is reaching toward
> a future of greater democracy and economic freedom. As it does so,
> our relationship will continue to broaden and deepen.[1]
>
> *Condoleezza Rice, Assistant to the President for*
> *National Security Affairs*

Throughout 2001 scholars of US-Russian relations on both sides of the Atlantic closely watched the foreign policies of the White House and the Kremlin. Many expected that President George W. Bush and his foreign and security policy team would implement a tough, possibly Reaganite-style hard line toward Russia led by a former KGB colonel. Their policy line toward Russia had less to do with a disdain for Putin, and was more indicative of an embrace of a 'market correction' to US-Russian relations. The administration had not permanently written off Russia, but preferred to downgrade the priority accorded to the relationship, waiting to re-invest in Russia at the bottom of the market. It was determined to conduct a serious dialogue with Russia, but only after expectations were lowered and relations had been re-balanced.

The first indications of such a posture surfaced during the election campaign and the early formation of the new administration's personnel and foreign policy. Those symptoms included: downgrading Russia in the US list of foreign policy priorities; the administration's harsh statements declaring its intention to withdraw unilaterally from the 1972 ABM treaty and to end strategic arms control negotiations with Russia; leveling charges against Russia as an active proliferator of critical WMD technologies (meaning mostly its cooperation with Iran in the nuclear energy sector); persistent criticism of Russia's method of resolving the domestic crisis in Chechnya (identified by President Vladimir Putin in 1999 as 'an anti-terrorist operation'); and accusing Moscow of suppressing freedom of speech (regarding the awkward use of legal and economic instruments to deprive the notorious oligarchs Gusinsky and Berezovsky of their media assets).

Top Russian policymakers, in their turn, accused the new US leadership of adventurous unilateralism in the world arena, of breaking down the structure of international treaties on strategic arms control and starting a new nuclear arms race, of interference in Russia's domestic affairs and of double-standards in the treatment of Russia.

Despite the fact that President Bush tried to establish, in his words, a 'frank and honest relationship' with the 'trustworthy' President Putin during the summits in Brdo and Genoa in June and July 2001, public opinion and the political and economic elites of the two nations were distressed. Americans experienced 'Russia fatigue', while Russians were disillusioned in their hopes for US expertise and help. Both nations were psychologically preparing for a disengagement, or even for another round of confrontation.

It seemed that US-Russian affairs reached a turning point on September 11, 2001, when Vladimir Putin placed a telephone call to George W. Bush to convey the Russians' condolences to the victims of the terrorist attacks against the Americans, and to assure the US president of Russia's full support for anti-terrorist counteractions.

Presidents Bush and Putin achieved further successes in encouraging a counter-terrorist coalition and securing the success of the fight against bin Laden's Al-Qaeda network in Afghanistan, avoiding a crisis over the US abrogation of the 1972 ABM treaty, and steadily improving Russia's overall relations with the West. It looked like the presidents had managed to end a dangerous deterioration of the bilateral relations that occurred during the 1990s and to change the course of US-Russian affairs from a series of nervous ups and downs to a stable, mutually beneficial ascent.

Yet the new US-Russian rapprochement rests on a very delicate basis: the personal relationship of the two national leaders. While this is very important for a genuine trust and better understanding, it cannot be sufficient for building a stable structure of bilateral relations. The Putin-Bush interaction cannot substitute for US-Russian relations. In this case, President Reagan's formula that 'It takes two to tango' should be read as a concert of nations, of political and business elites, not only of leading individuals.

During the year after 9/11, US-Russian relationships were in the 'courting' phase, as the two leaders cheered each other up with rhetorical bolstering. At the same time, the elites and the public were lagging behind the presidents in their visions, assessments and actions.

It appeared that the presidents had drawn certain lessons from the bilateral relations of the past two decades. The primary message was that each of the nations should learn to avoid Cold War-style harsh responses to any disagreements or contradictions, because emotional rhetoric prompted by instincts left over from the old days could seriously damage the fragile fabric of the new relationship. The Russian leadership demonstrates as much by its attitude to the establishing of the US military presence in Central Asia and Georgia – the regions of the Former Soviet Union (FSU) that are most sensitive for Russia – prior to the US-led counter-terrorist coalition operation in Afghanistan against bin Laden's Al-Qaeda network, as well as by the Kremlin's reserved reaction to the abrogation by the White House of the ABM Treaty and the decision to start deployment of a national missile defense. Moscow remained calm when Lithuania, Latvia and Estonia joined NATO. For its part, if the US administration had not acknowledged the difference between the first (1994–96) and the second (1999–2002) Chechen wars, it so far remained mum on the continued Russian 'anti-terrorist operation' in Chechnya.

All that time Putin was facing some domestic opposition to his policy of 'appeasing' Washington. Exploiting the widespread public anti-Americanism, certain groups among the Russian national security and foreign policy bureaucracy were cherishing their xenophobic suspicions towards the US and growing dissatisfied with the fact that Russia thus far had received little reward for its support of the domineering role of the US. They argued that Russia had shared vital intelligence with the CIA concerning North Korea, had withdrawn from the communication facilities in Cuba, and from the naval base at Cam Rahn Bay in Vietnam, but had received very little in return.

'The perpetuation of the antiterrorist war is fully in line with the new military doctrine of the United States, which centers on preemptive strikes against adversaries arbitrarily made up by the US itself', as Evgeny Primakov, former Russian prime minister, foreign minister and director of foreign intelligence, wrote in his recently published book.[2]

Critical voices were heard not only from the left flank, but from the conservative realists as well. Thus, leading political expert Vyacheslav Nikonov, summing up the diplomatic year 2002, stated that:

> ... the US withdrawal from the ABM treaty was a failure of the Russian foreign policy. In fact, we had no reason to support that decision, just as we had no reason to support NATO's expansion. Of course, this [NATO enlargement] is not a direct threat to the Russian security, but it is a creation of a European security system without our full participation in it.[3]

The dissent was heard even among Putin's men. 'The discussion of key military threats would be incomplete without mentioning the US invalidation of the 1972 ABM Treaty and the ongoing expansion of NATO', asserted Defense Minister Sergey Ivanov in an interview in December 2002. 'These steps do not pose an immediate threat to Russia's national security, [although] they undermine the existing strategic stability system'.[4]

However, President Putin managed to control the situation at least within his own ranks. The same Defense Minister, Sergey Ivanov, was quoted as saying that:

> ... the main threat to Russia's security is posed by terrorist groups active in the North Caucasus and Central Asia. To counter terrorist threats, we are maintaining close international ties within the antiterrorist coalition. We are ready for active ties with any country combating this evil.[5]

The Director of the Russian Foreign Intelligence Service, Sergey Lebedev, sounded even more in line with his president:

The main threats [to Russia] today come from international terrorism, organized crime and drug trafficking. The proliferation of weapons of mass destruction is also a major threat because we cannot be sure that maniacs will never assume control of such weapons. Ecological security is another vital task. No country in the world, not even the powerful USA, can stand up against these threats single-handed. We need to join forces.[6]

Skeptics within the Bush administration, while in retreat, rather than remain silent had precipitated a nuanced debate over the significance of Russia's contribution to the war on terrorism. They argued that Russia's support was inevitable because the US was doing Russia's bidding in rooting out terrorists in Central Asia.

Those voices were balanced in part by reasonable thinkers in the Capitol and in the White House. 'US-Russian cooperation in the war on terrorism' – in Condoleezza Rice's opinion – 'has been path-breaking in its breadth, depth, and openness. The passing of the ABM [1972 Anti-Ballistic Missile] Treaty and the signing of the Moscow Treaty reducing strategic arms by two-thirds make clear that the days of Russian military confrontation with the West are over.'[7]

In all, US-Russian relations were on an obvious ascent in 2002. Presidents George Bush and Vladimir Putin carried out successful summit meetings in Moscow and St. Petersburg in May and managed to sign a groundbreaking strategic arms reduction agreement. In addition, Russia was welcomed into NATO and given a seat on a council (though with a non-decisive voice). The US also was behind the pledge by the G-7 nations to contribute $20 billion over ten years to nonproliferation programs in Russia and the former Soviet republics and to give Russia a permanent seat at future G-8 meetings. The Bush administration lobbied Congress hard to grant Russia the status as a free-market economy; this was finally granted on 6 June 2002. Most important, the US and Russia have continued their cooperation in the war on terrorism.

As the US Ambassador to Russia, Alexander Vershbow, admitted:

The new NATO-Russia Council set up last year [2002] is another good example of how much the security environment has changed, and it underscores Russia's importance to meeting today's challenges. The NRC is off to an impressive start. Russia held a joint civil-emergency exercise with NATO Allies and Partners last fall in Noginsk, and also hosted a NATO-Russia seminar in Moscow two months ago on the military's role in combating terrorism. NATO and Russian military authorities in Brussels have completed joint assessments of the threat posed by

Al Qaeda to our troops in the Balkans and to civil aviation, and they have begun an assessment of the threat of proliferation of weapons of mass destruction.[8]

The Foreign Minister, Igor Ivanov, stated in December 2002:

From the viewpoint of possible consequences for our foreign policy and for the situation in the world as a whole I would put Russia's relations with the United States in the first place. This year we have managed to negotiate a very complex period connected with the Americans' unilateral withdrawal from the ABM treaty and not only to avoid sliding into confrontation, which for Russia would have entailed many unpleasant aspects, but even to maintain a constructive air of partnership. It was this that enabled us to move on within an extremely short period of time to the signing of a new treaty on the reduction of strategic offensive potentials, which provides real prospects for the next decade of reducing them by almost two-thirds, and to sign an important political declaration formulating the principles governing the relationship between our countries in the spheres that are the most important for Russia – the political, military, and economic. All this has enabled us to continue joint efforts in the fight against international terrorism, and not only in Afghanistan.[9]

The state of bilateral relations is also described positively in a reference note on the website of the Russian Foreign Ministry:

RUSSIAN-US RELATIONS

During the two years from September 2001 till September 2003 Presidents Putin and Bush met nine times in bilateral and multilateral formats, including President Putin's visit to the United States (November 12–15, 2001) and the reciprocal visit to Russia of President Bush (May 23–26, 2002). The last time the presidents met on June 1, 2003, during the celebrations to mark the tercentenary anniversary of St. Petersburg.

Prime Minister Mikhail Kas'yanov officially visited the United States during January 31 through February 4, 2002. The head of the Presidential Administration Alexander Voloshin visited Washington during February 23–26, 2003. Heads of the Russian governmental agencies visited the United States on official and business trips, among them Vice Prime Minister Alexey Kudrin, Minister of Agriculture Alexey Gordeev, Minister of Defense Sergey Ivanov, Minister of Economic Development Hermann Gref, Chairman of the Accounting Chamber Sergey Stepashin, Minister of the Press Mikhail Lesin, Minister of Fuel and Energy Igor Yusufov, Minster of Atomic Energy Alexander Roumyantsev, Minister of Transportation Sergei Frank, Minister of Communications Leonid Reyman, Head of the Federal Construction Committee Nikolai Koshman and others. Assistant to the President on National Security Condoleezza Rice, Secretary of Defense Donald Rumsfeld, the U.S. Trade Representative Robert Zoellick, as well as Secretaries of Commerce, Treasury, Energy, Justice and other departments visited Russia during the same period.

Contacts between the heads of the foreign policy agencies of the two countries were upheld on a permanent basis. During the period of interaction with the administration of President George W. Bush, Foreign Minister Igor Ivanov and Secretary of State Colin Powell met 35 times in bilateral and multilateral formats.

In the military political sphere efforts were focused on forming a new relationship in the strategic field on the principles of partnership and consideration of respective security interests based on the documents signed during the visit to Russia of President Bush (May 23–26, 2002) – the political Joint Declaration on the new strategic relationship between Russia and the USA, as well as the Strategic Offensive Reductions Treaty (effective since June 1, 2003).... We are in a process of working out definite agreements with the United States on specific measures for implementation of the initiative of the G8 summit (Kananaskis, June 2002) on Global Partnership Against the Spread of Weapons and Materials of Mass Destruction.

Cooperation is developing in the field of non-proliferation, first of all with regard to raising the effectiveness of the international control regimes – the Non-Proliferation Treaty (1968), CTBT, CWC, BWC, as well as missile technology non-proliferation. We have accumulated significant experience in the process of implementation of the program of assisting Russia in the annihilation of its WMD, disposal of strategic arsenals.

Russian-U.S. cooperation is also developing in resolving key international and regional issues, joint search for solutions to new global threats and challenges. Primarily it relates to the problem of international terrorism. The Joint Statement on anti-terrorist cooperation was signed by the presidents during the Moscow-St Petersburg (May 2002) summit. Issues pertaining to the fight against terrorism are regularly discussed by the Minister of Foreign Affairs and the Secretary of State.

A tested and efficient instrument of the bilateral cooperation in this field is the Russian-U.S. Working Group on fighting terrorism, which conducts regular meetings. The mandate of the Group is quite large and includes in particular issues related to countering terrorist nuclear and other WMD threats, coordinating activities in blocking the channels of financial support of terrorism (within the framework of implementation of UN SC Resolution 1373), as well as combating against illegal drugs trafficking as the major means of financial support for terrorist and extremist activities.[10]

Even the firm political stance shown by Russia during the eight weeks of an agonizing search for a compromise on the highest governmental level during the adoption of the UN Security Council Resolution 1441, which prevented the US from an unconditional war with Iraq – though it called on Iraq to submit to weapons inspections or face the threat of forced compliance – did not yet presuppose a serious crisis in the US-Russian relationship.

US officials were also rather optimistic about the future of bilateral relations. 'Whatever happens, I don't think the bilateral relationship between the United States and Russia will be strained to the breaking point', claimed Alexander Vershbow, the US Ambassador to Russia. 'Whatever the differences in our approach to the problem of Iraq, we have the same underlying goal'.[11]

In late January 2003 Putin announced that Moscow would toughen its line on Iraq should Baghdad fail to come clean on its weapons program. He also admitted the Kremlin did not want a confrontation with Washington over Iraq, prompting the influential daily *Kommersant* to assert that for Russia, 'America is more important than Iraq'.

However, the crisis developed when it became clear that Russia would veto the US-proposed UN resolution for an attack on Iraq. The confident claims by many US experts that Russia had no choice but to join the US against Iraq proved to be a faulty analysis.

The launching of the war against Iraq was seen in the US as part of a global war against terrorism. However, many in Russia saw the attack on Iraq as part of an effort by the US to monopolize the world petroleum markets and further its political and economic domination of the globe.

The Russian Foreign Ministry was the first to openly state its opposition to the 'aggressive' US policy against Iraq. Putin and his presidential staff seemed to be using Foreign Minister Ivanov as a sounding board both internationally and within Russia itself.

Then, in a major televised interview on 21 February 2003, Putin warned about a 'growing aggressiveness of influential forces in certain countries'. In his annual address to members of both houses of the Russian parliament on 16 May 2003, speaking about nuclear and terrorist threats, Putin made a remark that 'strong, well-armed national armies are sometimes used not to fight this evil [international terrorism] but to expand the areas of strategic influence of individual states', obviously pointing to the US-led operation in Iraq.

Why did the arch-realist Putin, who had worked so hard since September 11 to forge a bond with President Bush, choose to break ranks?

Foreign policy analysts and Russia-watchers singled out several reasons for that. The most obvious was *domestic public opposition* to the war conducted without the legitimate backing of the UN. Long before the operation in Iraq, Russian public opinion demonstrated rather widespread anti-American sentiment. An opinion poll of 500 city residents conducted by the Public Opinion Foundation–Gallup

International in October 2001 has shown that a total of 42.4 per cent of Muscovites approved of the US military efforts in Afghanistan, while 49.4 per cent disapproved of them; at least 32 per cent of Muscovites feared that the conflict would grow further and spill into other countries, including Russia. An overwhelming 60 per cent of the respondents believed that the US military action posed a threat to Russia, while 36.3 per cent of those polled opposed that opinion. More than half, 57 per cent, said that Russia must fully cooperate with the US, except in committing forces to action. At least 24.7 per cent advocated the position of a standby observer, while 11.3 per cent wanted Russia to denounce the US and demand a termination of the action.[12]

Leon Aron from the American Enterprise Institute provided an extended review of the Russian public attitude to the war in Iraq and in this relation to the US.[13] He pointed out that in a January 2003 national poll, 52 per cent of Russians felt 'indignant' about a possible US-British 'military operation against Iraq', while only three per cent approved of the idea.[14] Asked which side would enjoy their sympathy in the event of war, 50 per cent said neither, while ten percent would root for America and 32 per cent for Iraq.[15] While about one-fifth thought the US was preparing for war in order to 'destroy terrorist bases' or prevent Iraq from manufacturing weapons of mass destruction, twice as many ascribed America's bellicosity to a desire to 'show the world "who's the boss"', and over a third (34–37 per cent) considered US 'economic interests' – including control over Iraqi oil – as the underlying *casus belli*.[16]

In the months leading to war, positive attitudes toward America fell from 69 per cent in October 2002 to 48 per cent in March 2003, while negative ones rose from 24 per cent to 40 per cent.[17] With coalition forces massing in the Persian Gulf in early March, far more Russians considered the US a greater threat to world peace (71 per cent) than they did Iraq (45 per cent).[18]

By the end of March, as the coalition forces raced across the Euphrates plain, only 14 per cent of Russians believed that America played 'a mostly positive role in today's world';[19] 91 per cent disapproved of the war, while in another poll, 82 per cent expressed indignation over it.[20] President Bush commanded an all-time unfavorable 'high' of 76 per cent in Russia.[21] At the same time, Saddam Hussein's favorability ratings – at 22 per cent – barely budged with the outbreak of war, up a mere seven points from February 2002.[22] Similarly, in early March the majority of respondents (51 percent) felt that Iraq was neither a hostile nor a friendly country to Russia.[23]

Thus, most Russians' anger appears to have stemmed not from a sympathy with the target of American power but from its very exercise.

Despite their opposition to the war, the majority of Russians – when asked in polls between December 2002 and April 2003 which side their country should take – consistently replied that Moscow should remain neutral (61–73 per cent). Between seven and nine per cent advocated support for the US, while 19 to 32 per cent were for 'diplomatic assistance' to Iraq.[24]

Only one per cent of Russians believe that the US is a guarantor of peace in the world. The majority of respondents polled by the All-Russian Public Opinion Research Center in late April believe that the US interferes in the affairs of other countries, imposes its values on them (61 per cent) and is also trying to gain world dominance (61 per cent).[25]

A less articulated, though a quite important, reason for Putin's stance on the war in Iraq is *the Islamic factor*. Muslims account for 18 per cent of Russia's population. They live in the North Caucasus and in Bashkortostan and Tatarstan. The Tatars are, in fact, Russia's second largest nationality. Then there are six post-Soviet Muslim states on Russia's southern border: Azerbaijan, Kazakhstan, Kyrgyzstan, Tajikistan, Turkmenistan and Uzbekistan. Islam is now an integral part of politics within and around Russia. The US-led war against Iraq followed by a prolonged occupation could inflame the Muslim world and bring upheaval to Russia and its southern flank.

A series of research papers and memos prepared by Russian analysts after the NATO war against Yugoslavia emphasized the vital necessity of *preserving the United Nations Organization* as the only existing – although growing obsolete and demanding modern-ization – international instrument for settling inter-state disputes and maintaining the world order. And it seems that Putin truly adheres to this concept and persistently brings it to the floor. In his 2003 annual address to the Russian Federal Assembly the president devoted a significant part of his foreign policy analysis to the role and future of the United Nations:

The foundation of our foreign policy, the fundamental task of Russia's foreign policy, is the implementation of our national interests. And here, the basic principle continues to be the observance of the norms of international law. The events of the past year have once again demonstrated that guaranteeing national interests requires in equal measure both an effective diplomacy and a reliable Russian defense potential.

In today's world, the relations between states are determined to a considerable degree by the existence of serious, world-scale real and potential threats. Among such threats we include international terrorism, the proliferation of weapons of mass destruction, regional and territorial conflicts, and the drugs menace. In the event of an aggravated threat to the world community as a whole or to an individual country, it seems extremely important to have a decision-making mechanism which has to be comprehensible, transparent and recognized by everyone. It goes without saying that the United Nations and its Security Council are the most important such mechanism.

Yes, it is not always easy for the Security Council to pass a decision. Sometimes no decisions are passed. It happens sometimes that the initiators of a resolution do not have enough arguments to persuade other countries that their initiative is right.

Of course, UN decisions are far from being favored by everyone every time. But the world community has no other more universal mechanism. This mechanism should be looked after and maintained.

Of course, it is necessary to modernize the work of international organizations and to make it more effective. Russia is open to discussing these questions. I think that such approaches to international matters are civilized and correct.

These approaches are not directed against anyone or are in favor of anyone. It is our position, a position of principle, and we will adhere to it in the future.[26]

The next significant cause (not often mentioned by observers) of Putin's posture on the Iraqi war was closely related to the previous one. As Steven Sestanovich put it, 'he was *carried along by the French [and Germans]* into a more openly anti-American position than he expected. He found it a little hard to drop off their band-wagon'.[27] Moscow must have actually believed that France and Germany were ready to put up a serious opposition to the US to make them adhere to the UN charter. Very soon Putin discovered that both Chirac and Schroeder were pursuing their own, different goals, similar in only one way – both tried to improve their domestic political positions. A suspicion was also articulated that 'one of the goals of our European friends...has always been to prevent exces-sive rapprochement between Russia and the US, for such a develop-ment could strengthen the positions of both countries, especially that of Russia'.[28]

Many analysts agree that one more factor that influenced Putin's opposition to the US operation in Iraq was the abovementioned pressure from a part of the Russian ruling class, especially from the *national security bureaucracy.*

Finally, some scholars of Russian politics proposed the so-called *psychological reason.* They hint at a skeleton in Putin's closet: his habits and mindset of a security service officer have not died away; he is still suspicious of his Western partners and their intentions. His former colleagues from the intelligence service obviously reported to him varying assessments of the Bush team's global intentions published in the foreign press. For one example, see Anatol Lieven's article in the *London Review of Books* where he analyses what the US administration hopes to gain:

The planned war against Iraq is not after all intended only to remove Saddam Hussein, but to destroy the structure of the Sunni-dominated Arab nationalist Iraqi state as it has existed since that country's inception. The 'democracy' which replaces it will presumably resemble that of Afghanistan – a ramshackle coalition of ethnic groups and warlords, utterly dependent on US military power and utterly subservient to US (and Israeli) wishes.

Similarly, if after Saddam's regime is destroyed, Saudi Arabia fails to bow to US wishes and is attacked in its turn, then – to judge by the thoughts circulating in Washington think-tanks – the goal would be not just to remove the Saudi regime and eliminate Wahabism as a state ideology: it would be to destroy and partition the Saudi state. . . .

Beyond lies China. When the Bush Administration came to power, its major security focus was not the Middle East. . . . The greatest fears of right-wing nationalist gurus such as Robert Kagan concerned the future emergence of China as a super-power rival – fears lent a certain credibility by China's sheer size and the growth of its economy. As declared in the famous strategy document drawn up by Paul Wolfowitz in the last year of the first Bush Administration – and effectively proclaimed official policy by Bush Jr in his West Point speech in June – the guiding purpose of US strategy after the end of the Cold War should be to prevent the emergence of any 'peer competitor' anywhere in the world.[29]

Maybe knowing that, Putin, when asked at the press conference on 22 November 2002 whether the US had invited him to participate in or contribute to any military action in Iraq, avoided a direct answer. Instead he tried to draw attention to some other states of the Middle East and South Asia.

We should not forget about those who finance terrorism. Of the 19 terrorists who committed the main attacks on September 11th against the United States, 16 are citizens of Saudi Arabia, and we should not forget about that.

Now, where has Osama bin Laden taken refuge? They say that somewhere between Afghanistan and Pakistan. We know what Mr Musharraf is doing to achieve stability in his country and we are supporting him. But what can happen with armies armed with weapons that exist in Pakistan, including weapons of mass destruction, we are not sure on that aspect and we should not forget about that. And we agree with the President of the United States and his colleagues who say that we have to make sure that Iraq has no weapons of mass destruction in its possession.[30]

It seemed for a while that despite Condoleezza Rice's 'Forgive Russia' formula, the relationship was on a downhill slope again.

Some analysts in the US believed that Putin was 'in a genuinely awkward political position. He opposed the United States on Iraq, was ignored, showed himself to be basically irrelevant on the main issue of world politics, and he doesn't see an easy fix...there's no question that the personal relationship between the two presidents has already changed. There is a strong sense of disappointment in Putin'.[31]

But then on 1 June 2003 Presidents Bush and Putin signed a Joint Statement 'On The New Strategic Relationship', reaffirming the two nations' partnership and commitment to meet together the challenges of the twenty-first century.

What lessons can both nations and their respective leaderships learn from the experience of the last year?

It is not obvious what lessons were drawn by the Russian defense leadership. Defense Minister Sergey Ivanov seems to prefer to seek knowledge on the future of the Russian defense system from such sources as 'experienced experts and specialists', such as 'prominent senior commanding officers and veterans of the [Soviet] Armed Forces'. Defense Ministry mouthpiece *Krasnaya Zvezda* often quotes, for example, the last Soviet Minister of Defense, Marshal Dmitry Yazov, as such an expert on many issues of military reform.[32] During the US-led operation in Iraq he presented an analysis which might have prompted the Defense Ministry's erroneous advice to President Putin:

Iraqi soldiers resemble us when were fighting for Stalingrad...The moral, psychological and, consequently, combat characteristics of the soldiers of [the US-led] coalition are doubtful. They are so sensitive. And, look, how much junk they carry on themselves! We had been going into assault [during World War II]...throwing away our kit-bags and gas-masks – everything but our rifles. And we did not do badly. And here scantily clad Iraqi soldiers, fighting light, are thrashing the life out of the very well-equipped mercenaries...[33]

For Russia's political class, the lessons from the war in Iraq and Russia's diplomatic posture toward this war in the context of US-Russian relations had been formulated in a series of publications. Here is a summary of those conclusions:

- Russian policy lacked a clear strategic objective. It was not obvious whether we wanted to ensure that international law was observed, to save the UN Security Council, to befriend European states and play them off against the US, or to remain on good terms with America. Any of these objectives could be justified as part of an overarching strategy. But there was no strategy. And the absence of a strategy was not unique to this crisis – it was true of Russia's foreign policy as a whole.

- Russia's foreign policy was not very well-coordinated. At times Russia was clearly improvising and on occasions was clearly acting at cross-purposes.
- One of Russia's policy objectives has been and remains erroneous. It is counterproductive at the UN – even for tactical purposes – to attempt to play against its most powerful member. The UN ship is only barely afloat. It needs to be saved, rapidly repaired and modernized, and this should be done together with those whom we can sail on with.
- Out of slovenliness Russia simply did not look after its economic interests in Iraq. The government agencies did not try to prioritize those interests.
- The Russian intelligence services misled the Russian political leadership and the Russian political class deluded itself about Iraq's ability and readiness to fight.
- The Russian leadership must draw, without delay, this very import-ant conclusion: Russia's foreign policy must be consistently unpopular. Only then will it be able to meet genuine national interests of Russia. The Iraq war has demonstrated that an over-whelming majority of the Russian population, as well as a large part of the Russian elite, react to international events emotionally rather than objectively. Russia's foreign policy must become more pragmatic, as President Vladimir Putin repeatedly and justly says. This means that political developments in the world must be subject of a calm and non-biased analysis, occasionally defying Russian public opinion.[34]

The most obvious and important lesson for US foreign politics drawn from the American diplomatic efforts prior to and during the Iraq war is the one which is recognized both by the critics and proponents of US-Russian rapprochement: 'the Bush administration has not helped potential allies to understand its outlook and direc-tion, and without such understanding, friendly governments fear they are being led around by the nose'; 'the United States has failed to explain in clear terms to Russia its strategic objectives and interests'.[35]

NOTES

1. Condoleezza Rice, *A Balance of Power That Favors Freedom. U.S. Foreign Policy Agenda. An Electronic Journal of the U.S. Department of State*, Vol. 7, No. 4, Dec. 2002.

2. Yevgeny Primakov. 'The World After September 11' (Moscow: Mysl 2002) pp.135–6.

3. 'On the Whole, Russia Has Strengthened Its International Positions', interview with Dr Vyacheslav Nikonov, President of the Polity Foundation, Strana.Ru web site, Moscow, in Russian, 26 Dec. 2002, BBC monitoring. As quoted in CDI Russia Weekly, No. 238, 3 Jan. 2003.

4. Interfax news agency, Moscow, in English. 0849 GMT, 31 Dec. 2002. CDI Russia Weekly, No. 238, 3 Jan. 2003.

5. Ibid.

6. Interview with Colonel-General Sergey Lebedev, Director of Russia's Foreign Intelligence Service, *Rossiiskaya Gazeta*, 23 Dec. 2002.

7. Rice (note 1).

8. Alexander Vershbow, 'US-Russia Relations: Opportunities and Challenges in 2003', Moscow School of Political Studies Seminar, Perm, Russia, 27 Feb. 2003. Bureau of International Information Programs, accessed at <http://usinfo.state.gov/topical/pol/nato/03030601.htm> on 6 Sept. 2003.

9. *Rossiyskaya Gazeta*, 30 Dec. 2002.

10. *Russian-US Relations, reference data*, Official Internet site of the Russian Ministry of Foreign Affairs. 27 Aug. 2003, <www.ln.mid.ru/ns-rsam.nsf/1f773 bcd33ec925d432569e7004196dd/ 16dd0c29bd3ef47343256a2c0040bfb4?OpenDocument>.

11. Vershbow (note 8).

12. *Itar-Tass*, 9 Oct. 2001.

13. Leon Aron, 'Russia, America, Iraq', American Enterprise Institute/AEI Online (Washington), 1 May 2003. Accessed at <www.aei.org/include/pub_print.asp? pubID=17061> on 8 May 2003.

14. Vserossiyskiy Tsentr Izucheniya Obschestvennogo Mneniya (VTsIOM, Russian Center for Public Opinion and Market Research), conducted 24–27 Jan. 2003. Accessed at <www.russiavotes.org> on 6 March 2003.

15. Fond Obschestvennoye Mneniye (FOM, Public Opinion Foundation), conducted 1–2 Feb. 2003. Accessed at <www.fom.ru/virtual/body> on 6 March 2003.

16. VTsIOM, conducted 21–23 Sept. 2002. Accessed at <www.russiavotes.org> on 6 March 2003.

17. VTsIOM, conducted 26 Feb.–3 March 2003. Accessed at <www.wciom.ru> on 6 March 2003.

18. Ibid.

19. FOM, conducted 22 March 2003. Accessed at <www.fom.ru/reports/frames/of031201.html> on 19 April 2003.

20. FOM, conducted 22–23 March 2003. Accessed at <www.fom.ru/reports/frames/short/d031212.html> on 19 April 2003; and VTsIOM, conducted 21–24 March 2003. Accessed at <www.russiavotes.org/images/slide388.gif> on 22 April 2003.

21. FOM, conducted 29 March 2003. Accessed at <www.fom.ru/reports/frames/of031305.html> on 19 April 2003.
22. FOM, conducted 29 March 2003. Accessed at <www.fom.ru/reports/frames/of031304.html> on 19 April 2003.
23. Rossiyskoye Obschestvennoye Mneniye i Isledovaniye Rynka (ROMIR, Russian Public Opinion and Market Research), conducted 6–11 March 2003. Accessed at <www.romir.ru/socpolit/vvps/03_2003/iraq-war.htm> on 19 April 2003.
24. ROMIR, conducted Nov. 2002. Accessed at <www.romir.ru/socpolit/vvps/11_2002/iraq.htm> on 6 March 2003; FOM, conducted 1–2 Feb. 2003. Accessed at <www.fom.ru/virtual/body> on 6 March 2003; VTsIOM, conducted 24–27 Jan. 2003. Accessed at <www.russiavotes.org> on 6 March 2003; and VTsIOM, conducted 26 Feb.–3 March 2003. Accessed at <www.wciom.ru> on 6 March 2003.
25. Interfax, 15 May 2003.
26. Johnson's Russia List, No. 7186, 19 May 2003.
27. 'Expert Says US-Russian Strains May Not Be Easily Repaired', interviews with Stephen Sestanovich, Council on Foreign Relations George F. Kennan senior fellow in Russian and Eurasian studies on 12 May and again on 30 May 2003, CFR Publications. Accessed at <www.cfr.org/publication.php?id=6006> on 6 Sept. 2003.
28. Sergei Karaganov, 'Lessons of the Iraq War for Russia', paper for distribution at the conference 'Russia and the New World Architecture', organized by the *Russia in Global Affairs* journal on 12 May 2003 at the Hotel Baltschug Kempinski in Moscow.
29. Anatol Lieven, 'The Push for War', *London Review of Books*, Vol. 24, No. 19, 3 Oct. 2002. Accessed at <www.lrb.co.uk/v24/n19/liev01_.html> on 12 March 2003.
30. Remarks by President Bush and Russian President Putin in photo opportunity, Catherine Palace, St Petersburg, Russia on 22 Nov. 2002. Accessed at <www.whitehouse.gov/news/release/2002/11/print/20021122–2.html> on 28 Aug. 2003.
31. 'Expert Says US-Russian Strains May Not Be Easily Repaired', interviews with Stephen Sestanovich, Council on Foreign Relations George F. Kennan senior fellow in Russian and Eurasian studies on 12 May and on 30 May 2003. CFR Publications. Accessed at <www.cfr.org/publication.php?id=6006> on 6 Sept. 2003.
32. 'Armiya menyaet oblik' [Armed Forces Change its Character], *Krashaya Zvezda*, 22 April 2003; 'Yazov odobril reformu armii' [Yazov Approved the Armed Forces Reform], *Moskovskii Komsomolets*, 21 April 2003.
33. *Komsomolskaya Pravda*, 22 March 2003.
34. *The Moscow Times*, 25 April 2003; *Vedomosti*, 22 April 2003.
35. Stephen Sestanovich, 'Restoring US-Russia Harmony', *The Washington Post*, 31 May 2003; 'Curt Weldon: Jackson-Vanick Amendment is to be Abrogated by September', *Izvestia*, 29 July 2003.

Military Reform in Russia and the Global War Against Terrorism

ALEXANDER GOLTS

Reform of the Russian military is required for two reasons: the armed forces' lack of modern equipment, and its growing internal social problems. Fixing these problems will require adjustments at several levels: in funding, in military education, in eliminating corruption and arbitrariness, and in overcoming "old thinking" associated with a Cold-War mentality. Recent statements by the Russian Minister of Defense stating that "military reform is over" cannot help but make one pessimistic about the future of military reform in Russia.

The need for fundamental military reform has been clear since 7 May 1992 – the day the Russian armed forces were officially established following the collapse of the Soviet Union. No one could dispute that a Soviet-type military organization stood in total opposition to a market economy and democratic society. Since then there have been at least two attempts to initiate large-scale reforms (the first one was announced by Pavel Grachev in 1992 and the second by Igor Sergeev in 1997). Both failed. Now the Kremlin is trying to launch a third attempt. President Vladimir Putin recently cited military reform as one of three top national priorities (together with doubling the GDP and fighting poverty). This is more than understandable. The unreformed armed forces have become one of the most serious obstacles to President Putin's modernization plans.

The Russian president now faces two challenges in defense and security. The first is that the Russian armed forces do not meet any modern requirements. Top military officials try to reduce the problem down to the need to rearm the armed forces with new precision weapons and other equipment. Russian Defense Minister Sergey Ivanov insisted in 2001 that the first priority in military reform is rearmament, which had to begin with modernization of the Space

Forces. Many independent experts doubt seriously that the Russian military-industrial complex is capable of producing modern weapons. But even if a miracle was to happen and the Russian army received this equipment, it would not be able to use it effectively. The war in Chechnya has shown how inefficient is this military concept in a period of local conflicts.

The second challenge is that the unreformed armed forces have become Russia's most urgent social problem. Decay is the best word to describe the situation. Young men look on army service as state slavery and try to avoid it. Military officials repeatedly complain that they are able to draft less then 11 per cent of those who are supposed to be conscripts. As a result, most recruits meet neither health nor intelligence standards. At the same time, the military fails to man units with the planned number of soldiers. Desertion is now epidemic. Soldiers are deserting in platoons and companies. According to official statements, there are now more then 2,265 deserters (unofficially, the military believes that the number is several times higher). These young people who have left their units with weapons have quickly became criminals. In 2001, deserters killed a general who tried to stop them. Some observers have written about the possibility of a new '"Ironclad" Potemkin' revolt.

Soldier morale is extremely low. Military commanders are powerless to stop *dedovschina* (daily severe hazing of first-year soldiers by those in the second year). Military prosecutor general Alexander Savinkov stated that 1,200 military men from all the 'power ministries' became so-called 'non-combat losses' during the first eight months of 2003. He admitted that 16 soldiers were killed during hazing.[1] Defense Minister Sergey Ivanov had previously reported that 531 servicemen were killed in a ten-month period in 2002 as a result 'of crimes and incidents', and 20,000 men were badly injured.[2]

Nor is it only soldiers who don't want to serve – neither do junior officers. In 2002 more than half the officers who left the armed forces did so early. This deterioration continues, even though the president had redeemed all his promises to the armed forces. Since 1999 the defense budget has grown more than three times – rising from 109 billion rubles to 346 billion (in 2003). However, no positive changes have come about: the level of combat readiness and discipline is just as low as it was few years ago. All of this means that the Russian armed forces are not ready to defend the country and that, at the same time, they are also dangerous for Russia. Top military personnel demonstrate neither the will nor the ability to effect fundamental changes.

The global war on terrorism added a very important international dimension to military reform in Russia. Before September 11, 2001, western democracies had only a 'negative' interest in Russian military reform. The US and alliances were interested that the vestiges of the huge Soviet military machine never again become a threat to the West. Now a new question arises: can the Russian army become a real partner of the US armed forces, and can Russian military units be integrated into the American military machine? Or, looking at the problem from a Moscow perspective, can Russia utilize this unique opportunity, when its ability to conduct joint operations with the US armed forces can be very important to Washington?

A NEW DEADLOCK

If we compare these new military reform plans with the previous ones, we easily find reasons for optimism. Two years ago Russia's top military leadership refused even to examine the possibility of comprehensive military reform and were instead content to muddle through with reorganizations and reductions. For example, the 'Plan for Armed Forces Structuring to 2005' significantly reduced the number of service personnel and directed a handful of organizational changes. The latter included merging military districts, separating the Space Forces from the Strategic Rocket Forces, combining the Air Force with the Air Defense Troops and the re-establishment of a General Command for Ground Troops.[3] It is striking that for years prior to this plan, the integration of the Space Forces and the Strategic Rocket Forces, and the elimination of the General Command for Ground Troops had been held up as important innovations in the process of military reform. In fact, these 'reforms' represent nothing more than victories by one clan of military bureaucrats over another.[4] The single positive result of all this activity has been a real reduction in the numbers of troops. However, this has been achieved without any real gains in the efficiency or preparedness of Russia's armed forces.

On 10 July 2003, the Russian government adopted the 'Special Federal Program to Transform the Staffing of the Armed Forces Primarily by Contract Servicemen'. In spite of Defense Minister

Sergey Ivanov's promises, the program has so far not been published. To analyze this we must rely on a few interviews with top
MOD officials. According to those interviews, 80 permanent combat-
ready units (in which 147,500 privates and sergeants serve) must
transition from conscription to 'contract' (all-volunteer) troops. The
transition is scheduled to begin in the latter part of 2003 and should
be completed by 2007.[5] Of these units, 72 units are from the armed
forces, five are from the Internal Troops, and three are from the
Border Guard Troops. Putin even pushed Ivanov to acknowledge
that the first step in reform needs to be the establishment of a professional corps of non-commissioned officers (NCOs). Ivanov even
promised that 'professional' sergeants will begin to appear in all
Russian units as early as 2004. The MOD also plans to enlist
citizens of CIS countries. For Russians, the main incentive will have
to be money (a private in the 'new' units is promised a salary of
6,369 rubles – which is more than company commanders in 'standard'
units receive). The MOD also proposed giving post-service solders
benefits that would allow them to enter the best Russian universities.
The possibility of receiving Russian citizenship is supposed to be
a good motivation for immigrants from the CIS.

It is clear that at the end of the day Vladimir Putin has managed
to persuade top military brass to make military reform a cornerstone
effort. Nevertheless, most Russian observers have already concluded
that this attempt to fundamentally reform Russia's armed forces will
fail – as all previous attempts in recent history have failed.

First of all, there is no guarantee that the program will be implemented. Its 'blueprint' as presented by the MOD on 24 April was
different from the final version. The military planned the transition
of 209 units (176,000 NCOs and privates). They wanted to switch to
all-voluntary status not only MOD units (ground forces – 79 units;
navy – 7 units; airborne troops – 5 units), but also Border Guard
Troops – 83 units, Interior Troops – 5 units, Railroad Troops – 28 units,
as well as some units of the special contracting service, and the
Federal Agency of Governmental Communication and Information
(FAPSI)[6]. The MOD asked for 138 billion rubles to implement the
program, but an interdepartmental commission adopted a different
figure – 79.1 billion. MOD leaders are looking for any cause to stop
the program. The military insist that any additional cut would stop
the program forever. There is no doubt that they will use any delay
in financing to advocate the rejection of the transition to all-volunteer

units. It is entirely symptomatic that Defense Minister Sergey Ivanov revealed that he personally was not certain that the MOD would be able to find 170,000 volunteers.

But the main defect of the federal program resides in its basic principles. The general goal of the program is the constructing of a 'mixed army' – partly all-volunteer and partly conscripted armed forces at the same time. This model can be accepted as a temporary option – on the assumption that the government will gradually replace units formed by conscription with all-volunteer units. But the goals of the concept are totally different. Ivanov has insisted that the 'mixed model' would be preserved forever.[7] The military insist that the conscription system must be preserved in order to maintain a so-called 'mobilization reserve' – the hypothetical ability to call up from six to eight million reservists during a war.

But this means that no serious changes in structure, organization or buildup are needed. The conscript system justifies preserving the top-heavy structure of the officer corps. Defense Ministry officials explain that Russia needs a surplus of senior officers who are pre-pared to command the divisions of reservists. On a related point, retaining the draft means that there is no need to change dramatic-ally the system of military education in which officers give draftees only the most elementary military training. And finally, the conscript system is used to justify retention of other types of 'mobilization capacities', including controls over industrial and procurement enterprises. These controls result in Defense Ministry officials exer-cising a selfish trusteeship over certain industries, thereby prevent-ing them from operating efficiently according to market influences. Last but not least, as long as the draft is preserved, the General Staff need not fundamentally rework its strategies and plans for the country's defense.

Thus, the federal program on transition to contract units can hardly result in the appearance of a new modern armed forces in Russia. But maybe the country can at least get a few combat-ready units? In my view that's more than doubtful. The specific culture of conscript armed forces will not permit raising even a few profes-sional units.

MOD officials pretend they see no difference between profes-sionals and mercenaries. Authors of the federal program focus only on the ability to pay salaries and improve social conditions of soldiers. They simply ignore the vital need for radical changes in military training and education. The top brass see no difference between professional NCOs, who have military service experience and special training, versus conscripts who have been drilled in training schools for less than six months. Such sergeants will have neither the knowledge nor the experience that can help them win authority in barracks. Their arrival within the armed forces will not change the situation with discipline.

As a consequence, discipline in 'contract' units will be as low as in conscript units. As if foreshadowing this result, Ivanov announced that the first 'contract' regiment of paratroops of the 76th Airborne Division will be trained using the same methods used for training conscripts. 'Once the paratroops regiment has been 100-percent manned with contract servicemen, the personnel will undergo individual training for the first six months of the training process, as well as developing the subunits' teamwork and coordination within the squad, platoon, company, and battalion. Over the next six months the readiness of the regiment in question to perform combat missions effectively in "hot spots" will be tested under real conditions, in this case the Chechen Republic', insisted Ivanov.[8]

A regiment trained in this way will hardly be more effective at fighting a war in Chechnya than conscript units. Moreover, the officers will have less influence over *kontraktniks* (soldiers serving voluntarily under contract) than over conscripts. Battle-experienced officers have explained privately that they expect to face greater difficulties in forcing contract units made up of fully mature men to risk their lives in battle situations than in forcing a group of 18-year-olds to do the same. (Of course, no one among this group draws a connection between low levels of command authority and inadequate professional training.) It came as no surprise that discipline and morale in the 76th Division's 'contract' regiment are very low. More then 500 soldiers canceled their contracts after they understood that in a few months they would have to go to Chechnya.[9] In the end, the generals will likely have every reason to declare that an all-volunteer army is a poor idea for Russia. They will argue that professionals are more expensive than a conscript army, but not more effective. If the Defense Ministry manages to preserve the draft, it doesn't matter how many *kontraktniks* serve in the military, even some special units will never attain a professional status and character.

There is no doubt that the MOD and the General Staff are trying to preserve the draft as long as possible. A reduction in the number of conscripts is possible only after 50–60 per cent of the army is made up of *kontraktniks*, according to General-Colonel Vasiliy Smirnov, Chief of the Main Organizational-Mobilization Directorate of General Staff.[10] (Military officials anticipate that only 15 per cent of the armed forces will be staffed with volunteers by 2008.) Top military authorities have a clear objective – they want to use *kontraktniks* to overcome the 'demographic hole' that is anticipated to open between 2006 and 2008. (According to Smirnov's predecessor, General-Colonel Vladislav Putilin, the population decline in Russia will soon mean a real shortfall of young, conscript-eligible males. If nothing is done, Russia's armed forces, its security ministries and other related agencies will find themselves with only 49–53 per cent of the necessary recruits.)[11] Already it is rather easy to predict the outcome of the current reform effort: in the end the military will report that the country does not have enough resources to support an all-voluntary military organization.

MOVING IN THE OPPOSITE DIRECTION

The transition to an all-volunteer service is very important but not the only element of military reform. The reform must include radical changes in military education and in the system of officer service. If for Russian conscripts military service is a form of legal-ized slavery, for officers it approximates to the institution of serfdom. They retain the formalities of autonomy and professionalism but are in reality locked into a system characterized by arbitrariness and patronage. Unless an officer has support from some high-placed official, his fate is entirely in the hands of his immediate commander and officials in the personnel department. Without having to justify their decisions, these people can choose to promote an officer or keep him where he is. They can send him to Moscow, or to some godforsaken post on the Chinese border. Colonel-General Pankov admitted that there is no mechanism in place to review appointments or to correct 'mistakes'. He also admitted that the promotion process in the armed forces does not function according to principles of open competition.[12]

However, if the appointment process were made more transparent, military commanders (not to mention personnel department officials) would lose an important lever of power and authority – and frankly speaking, their biggest source of bribes.

As with the transition to all-volunteer service, the MOD demonstrates bureaucratic activity and sabotage at the same time. Top military officials accept that the military education system needs major changes. On 27 May 2002, the Russian government adopted a federal program of military education reform. According to the program, the research must be concluded and proposals for reform for the period 2003–05 be submitted.[13] But the changes proposed run totally counter to the goal of raising the professionalism of Russian military officers. The MOD is trying to overcome officer-corps problems in the typical Soviet bureaucratic way. They want to halt the current exodus of junior officers and of cadets in military academies.

First, they propose increasing the service time of the officer's first contract from five to ten years, which would prevent junior officers from leaving the armed forces. The MOD also plans to force cadets wishing to leave military academies to pay at least 500,000 rubles for their education.

Second, MOD leaders want to lower, rather than raise, the level of education. Insisting that their goal is to concentrate on officer professionalism, they plan to reduce the educational period from five to four years. It is clear that they want to reject all liberal education. They want to preserve the situation in which, to borrow from Samuel Huntington's terminology, the Russian military officer is less of an 'expert in the management of violence', and more of a 'military hand-worker', whose knowledge is limited to the use of one or two weapons systems. The cynical estimation is that such 'specialization' would not allow military officers to find good positions in the civil sector. Thus, they would have no other choice but to stay in the armed forces.

The professionalism of Russian officers is very specialized – it is the ability to give the mass of conscripts primitive military training and then to deploy it on the battlefield. Contrary to all other modern armed forces, the foundation of the Russian army is not the skill of its officer corps, but a poorly-trained mass of conscripts, the effectiveness of which consists mainly in the ability to replenish itself constantly. Thus we can hardly predict that professional units could appear in the foreseeable future.

AGAINST THE TRADITIONAL ENEMY

Another important question – does the Russian military desire to cooperate with the US against terrorism or not? After the September 11,

2001 tragedy, Russia claimed to be the US' strongest ally in the anti-terrorist coalition. But this did not lead to serious changes in military planning or training. Nothing changed even after the hostage-taking in Moscow when President Putin ordered amendments to the 'National Security Concept' to reorient Russia's armed forces toward fighting terrorism.[14] But Ivanov made no attempt to hide his skepticism about the need for such a reorientation. He stated:

In my view, it is still premature right now to speak of the specific content of changes to Russia's defense priorities, and to the functions and tasks of its armed forces in connection with the threat posed by international terrorism. [. . .] No radical revision of the fundamental principles governing the operation of the armed forces is required. Requisite changes will have to be made to the content of the principal normative documents when it comes to ensuring the state's military security, including the Russian Federation National Security Concept. [. . .] I think in the work of revising the tasks not only of the armed forces, but also of the entire state military organization in peacetime, principal attention should focus on areas such as intelligence and notification, defense and protection of the state border, the communications system, key facilities in the national infrastructure, as well as preparing forces and systems for operating in emergency situations.[15]

To date, military thinkers in Russia have not tried to answer the questions raised by the global war against terrorism. Are the existing organizational forms of the armed forces adequate for responding to the so-called asymmetrical threat? Are there any differences between anti-terrorist warfare and traditional anti-guerrilla war? If the differences are not so crucial, how does one escape all the hardships connected with long occupations of foreign territories? Are crucial changes in troop training needed to make them ready to fight against a non-traditional enemy?

Only the Main Staff of Airborne Troops tried to develop the president's ideas. The Staff plans to stand up several fully-equipped battalions together with a transport aviation wing. The plan calls for these units to maintain 12-hour readiness.[16] However, it looks as though all these proposals are buried in a bureaucratic battle between Chief of the General Staff Anatoly Kvashnin and Georgy Shpak, Commander-in-Chief of the Airborne Troops. All attempts to integrate 'anti-terrorist' elements into military exercise scenarios look artificial. The last such attempt was undertaken this summer during the strategic exercise 'Vostok – 2003'. Commander-in-Chief of the Russian Navy, Admiral Victor Kuroedov, did not try to hide his dissatisfaction, summing up the results of the exercises as follows: 'The first decision of the Staff was directed at unleashing war in the region, not at stabilizing the situation'.[17] To be sure, one can hardly imagine how to marry the capabilities of missile cruisers and nuclear attack submarines with anti-terrorist attacks, since the former are built only to fight against aircraft carriers groups. But very few generals are even ready to think about this. 'Vostok – 2003' was the first attempt at 'new thinking' in the military sphere.

One can expect that the Russian General Staff is now preoccupied with plans for reforming the armed forces in order to ready them for anti-terrorist operations, as well as with plans for possible cooperation with US troops in anti-terrorist activity in CIS countries, if not elsewhere. But that is not happening. General-ColonelYuri Baluyevskiy, First Deputy of the General Staff, and in my view one of the smartest and most non-conformist of Russian generals, expressed total dissatisfaction with the results of the NATO-Russian conference held last December [2002]. Baluyevskiy insisted that in all the reports only general phrases prevailed.[18]

But it cannot be otherwise, because the Russian military feel humiliated whenever they are asked to take the Chechen or Afghan conflicts as models for future wars. Russian generals are really humiliated when someone insists that future wars have a local character, and that the center of gravity in such an operation will move to the Air Force.

But against whom will Russian generals train their troops, if not against terrorists? Their statements leave no room for doubt. 'The US and some other NATO countries try to use threat of terrorism to cover their far-reaching geopolitical goals', writes prominent Russian military theoretician and President of the Academy of Military Science Army, General Makhmud Gareev, in his article 'What Kind of Armed Forces Does Russia Need?' And his answer: 'Orientating the armed forces only toward low-intensity conflicts and local wars or only for the war on terrorism is rather dangerous. Such an orientation in the structuring and training of the armed forces could lead to a deterioration of the army, the fleet and the officer staff'.[19]

On 15 January 2003, the annual session of the Academy of Military Sciences was held in Moscow, with the Defense Minister and Chief of the General Staff in attendance. Top army commanders and military theorists tried to prove that a source of future conflicts will be the US' desire to control oil-rich regions. They did not rule out the possibility that Russia would confront the US in these conflicts. The Chief of the Main Operations Directorate, General-Colonel Alexander Rukshin, spoke about modernizing the command-and-control system. He complained that the existing system has only a limited defense against precision weapons. Only the US and Western countries have precision weapons. In his presentation, the Chief of the Navy Staff, Admiral Victor Kravchenko, stated that the main threat to Russia today and for the future is the US Navy's ability to destroy thousands of targets inside Russia using only conventional warfare.[20]

It is not just a matter of wording. Since the Russia-Belarus Zapad '99 [West '99] maneuvers, the Russian armed forces have been using a single scenario during military exercises, both for the European and Asian theaters. According to that scenario, the armed forces only have sufficient resources to prevent an enemy from penetrating Russia in the event of aggression. As for stopping the aggression, the idea is that that can only be achieved by means of nuclear weapons. To that end, strategic bombers would deliver a 'demonstration strike' using cruise missiles with some nuclear warheads – striking targets in deserts or thinly populated areas on the enemy's territory. After that, according to the theory, the aggressor would fear a full-scale nuclear war and consent to negotiations. If that did not happen, a strike with strategic missiles with nuclear warheads would be made. The General Staff has made no plans beyond that: understanding that the start of a full-scale nuclear war means the end of the world. Most recently, this scenario was drilled in the course of a command-staff exercise from 7–13 October 2002. At the final stage of the exercise, there were a number of successive strikes from strategic bombers and launches of three strategic nuclear missiles.

Ironically, each time something happens to show how far removed these scenarios are from the real threats to Russian security. A few weeks after 'Zapad '99' had concluded, detachments of Chechen warlords invaded Dagestan, and it took a month to deploy troops from Russia. On 9/11 Russia was conducting exercises. The American military had to call Moscow asking that the exercises be stopped. In 2002 Chechen terrorists took hostages in the center of Moscow a week after the strategic exercises ended.

It is a real mystery why Russian military commanders prefer to train the armed forces against a virtual rather than a real adversary. Many US analysts insist these anti-Western perceptions are the result of the Cold War. I find it hard to share such views. After all, Russian generals understand that there is no chance of 'imperialist aggression'. Two thousand deployed warheads still have a deterrent effect. The example of North Korea speaks for itself.

The Russian General Staff only pretend that it is seriously preparing for war against the US and the West. The most important part of the strategic exercises I mentioned before was not the launching of the ballistic missiles. For MOD and General Staff planners the most important aspect was the attempt to call up reservists. As a main achievement of 2002 Ivanov pointed to the mobilization of 7,500 reservists and their transport a few thousand kilometers. The mobilization of reservists was the most important element of the 'Vostok – 2003' exercises.

Why are these mobilizations so important when the Russian armed forces lack the resources to train enlisted military personnel? Only a global threat could justify maintaining an armed force numbering 1.1 million men, the current conscription system and an additional reserve of many millions. The rash reductions in the size of the armed forces that began in 1992 triggered a furious reaction from Russia's military elite. They realized full well that the Soviet model can function effectively only by preserving its character as a multi-million-man force. The need to maintain a so-called multi-million 'mobilization resource' in turn justifies a conscript service. The generals insist that, as a result, the number of reservists will decrease considerably, and that it will be not possible to draft millions of soldiers in the event of a large-scale war threat. However, the military authorities intentionally ignored the fact that the strategic stocks of arms, munitions and foodstuffs needed to equip a multi-million-man army have long been exhausted. If new objectives were to be set for the Russian armed forces, this entire structure would become pointless. And the generals are defending the Soviet-style military system. The need for radical military reforms will become evident as soon as the armed forces start changing their orientation away from opposition to NATO and the US, and toward carrying out specific anti-terrorist objectives.

WHAT HAS TO BE DONE

So any quick positive changes in the Russian armed forces are hardly possible. The Russian military simply cannot imagine another military organization other than one based on conscription and on total oppression of military personnel. Those who think changes are important had best prepare for a long period of work to enlighten the Russian elite. Achieving the enlightenment of the military and civil elite is a central priority for those who consider military reform a major task for the coming decades, not years.

First, it will be necessary to write a real, demythologized military history of Russia and the USSR, starting with World War II. It will be necessary to familiarize junior officers and military school cadets with other models of military organization and maintenance, and to expose them to the experiences of other countries with well-organized, professional militaries. We need to begin now to educate the next generation of teachers in military academies and 'experts' in the fields of a military history, strategy, military administration, and the theory and practice of the civil-military relations according to a different and broader set of ideas and principles.

Naturally, this process will take a lot of time and money. But, in my opinion, it is the only way to halt the automatic reproduction of existing militarist attitudes.

NOTES

1. <www.fcinfo.ru>, 3 Sept. 2003.
2. RIA–*Novosti*, 26 Nov. 2002.
3. *The Russian Journal*, 16 Sept. 2000.
4. Itogi 30, 1997.
5. *Izvestia*, 11 July 2003.
6. 'Chasti postoyannoy gotovnosti VS RF planiruetsya perevesti na kontraktnuyu osnovu', Strana.ru, 15 April 2003..
7. RIA – *Novosti*, 11 July 2003.
8. *Rossiyskaya Gazeta*, 14 Jan. 2003.
9. Interfax-AVN,1 Aug. 2003.
10. *Izvestiya*, 5 Feb. 2003.
11. *Yezhenedel'nyy zhurnal*, 13, 2002
12. *Krasnaya zvezda*, 9 Jan. 2003.
13. <http://www.government.ru/data/news_print.html?he_id = 103&news_id>.
14. Interfax, 28 Oct. 2002.
15. *Rossiyskaya gazeta*, 14 Jan. 2003.
16. Interfax-AVN, 5 Aug. 2003.
17. *Russkii kurier*, 30 Aug. 2003.
18. *Moskovskyy komsomolets*, 9 Jan. 2003.
19. *Otechestvennye zapiski*, 8, 2003.
20. *Nezavisimaya gazeta*, 31 Jan. 2003.

The US Military Engagement in Central Asia and the Southern Caucasus: An Overview

RICHARD GIRAGOSIAN

The regions of Central Asia and the Southern Caucasus have each acquired an elevated strategic importance in the new security paradigm of post-September 11th. Comprised of five states, Kazakhstan, Kyrgyzstan, Tajikistan, Turkmenistan and Uzbekistan, Central Asia's newly enhanced strategic importance stems from several other factors, ranging from trans-national threats posed by Islamic extremism, drug production and trafficking, to the geopolitical threats inherent in the region's location as a crossroads between Russia, Southwest Asia and China. Although the U.S. military presence in the region began before September 11th, the region became an important platform for the projection of U.S. military power against the Taliban in neighboring Afghanistan.

Similarly, the Southern Caucasus, commonly referred to as the Transcaucasus, has long served as a key arena for competing regional powers. For much of the past two centuries, the Transcaucasus has been hostage to the competing interests of the dominant regional actors: Russia, Turkey and Iran. And this historical legacy is matched by the realities and vulnerabilities of the current security situation in the region. The three states of the Transcaucasus, Armenia, Azerbaijan, and Georgia, each face a difficult course of economic and political reform, systemic transition and nation building in a struggle to overcome the legacy of seven decades of Soviet rule.

These two strategic regions also play important roles as "security sentries" along the front line of a dynamic U.S. engagement in response to the emergence of new non-state security threats. But both regions also face more fundamental internal challenges, ranging from an overall deficit of democracy, and the related predominance of "strongmen over statesmen," to economic mismanagement and widespread corruption. These factors significantly impede the reform efforts of these states in transition, and seriously erode the still fragile security environment. It is this set of internal factors that presents the most daunting challenge, however, as the core fragility of these states cannot be effectively overcome simply through policies relying on enhancing their security or military capabilities.

OVERVIEW: THE SOUTHERN CAUCASUS AND CENTRAL ASIA

The Southern Caucasus, commonly referred to as the Transcaucasus, has long served as a key arena for competing regional powers. For much of the past two centuries, the Transcaucasus has been hostage to the competing interests of the dominant regional actors: Russia, Turkey and Iran. And this historical legacy is matched by the realities and vulnerabilities of the current security situation in the region. The three states of the Transcaucasus – Armenia, Azerbaijan and Georgia – each face a difficult course of economic and political reform, systemic transition and nation-building. The region also continues to struggle in overcoming the legacy of constraints and challenges stemming from seven decades of Soviet rule.

The pronounced vulnerability of the Transcaucasus has been further compounded by a set of low-intensity conflicts and new security threats related to a serious weakening of state power and a real potential for state failure. The most recent security threats are posed by cases of 'conflict spillover' in Georgia's lawless Pankisi Gorge and from conflict-prone southern Russia, and from broader shortcomings in the now looming process of political succession.

Similarly, the region of Central Asia has also acquired a new strategic importance in recent years. Comprised of five states (Kazakhstan, Kyrgystan, Tajikistan, Turkmenistan and Uzbekistan) Central Asia has emerged as a region of strategic importance given its vast energy resources, its regional threats of narcotics production and trafficking, and its geographic location. It is the geography of Central Asia, however, that has contributed most to making the region both a short-term and a longer-term security priority to US national interests.

Its proximity to Afghanistan was crucial in planning and operations against the Taliban in neighboring Afghanistan, endowing the central Asian region with elevated strategic importance in the new security paradigm of post-September 11. Although the US military presence in the region was well established long before September 11, the region became an important platform for the projection of US military power in Operation 'Enduring Freedom'.

The Central Asian states also continue to play an important role as 'security sentry' for the ongoing stabilization effort in Afghanistan and to better position US forces in the medium-term safeguarding of stability in Pakistan. Over the longer-term, Central Asia's strategic importance stems from several other factors, ranging from transnational threats posed by Islamic extremism, drug production and trafficking, to the geopolitical threats inherent in the region's location as a crossroads between Russia, Southwest Asia and China.

Both these regions also face more fundamental internal challenges, ranging from an overall deficit of democracy, and the related predominance of 'strongmen over statesmen', to economic mismanagement and widespread corruption. These factors significantly impede the reform efforts of these states in transition, further contributing to a significant loss in state power. It is this set of internal factors that presents the most daunting challenge, however, as the core fragility of these three states cannot be effectively overcome simply through policies relying on enhancing their security or military capabilities.

The core focus of Western policies in the region over the past decade has largely been driven by considerations related to the development of their energy reserves and the challenges of securing export routes amid the competing interests of the regional powers. This long-standing energy focus has now been superseded by a pursuit of security and stability, within the prism of the global fight against terrorism. There has been a fundamental and sweeping change in US policy in the region underway for some time, however.

The foundation for current US policy in the Transcaucasus rests with the new strategic partnership between the US and Russia. But as Russia reasserts its position in Central Asia, the region, as well as the Caucasus, may very well emerge as the next arena in this mounting competition between Moscow and Washington, making the quest for stability and self-sufficiency among the infant states in the region even more important.

THE COURSE OF US ENGAGEMENT IN CENTRAL ASIA

Pre-September 11

In the period immediately following the collapse of the Soviet Union and the subsequent emergence of the newly-independent states in 1991, US policy toward Central Asia centered on a security relationship with Kazakhstan. This initial focus on Kazakhstan stemmed in large part on the need to secure the Kazakh nuclear

arsenal and, in December 1993, resulted in the signing of a cooperative threat reduction (CTR) agreement to dismantle and destroy the
country's more than 100 SS-18 missiles.

By 1994, the US cemented its bilateral security cooperation with
Kazakhstan through a defense cooperation agreement that forged
new cooperation in defense doctrine and training. The neighboring
states of Kyrgyzstan, Turkmenistan and Uzbekistan also joined
Kazakhstan in entering NATO's Partnership for Peace Program
(PfP). Central Asian membership in the NATO PfP served as the
main avenue for Western security engagement and a number of
officers from these states, as well as from Tajikistan, participated in
PfP exercises by 1995. The US-Kazakh defense relationship was
expanded in 1995 to include deeper cooperation in nuclear security
and defense conversion efforts.

The US approach to Central Asia was also driven by overarching
geopolitical considerations, with an underlying goal of containing
the influence of China, Iran and Russia. The promotion of Turkey as
a key US proxy force in the region was also designed to bolster

Figure 1. The strategic Arena: Central Asia and the South Caucasus.

US geopolitical objectives, although widespread disappointment and frustration among the Central Asian states over Turkey's failure to meet their early expectations significantly limited Turkish appeal and influence in the region.

Another core element in US policy throughout the 1990s was the danger of proliferation, as well as the need for regional security. As with Kazakhstan, the US entered into a bilateral security relationship with Uzbekistan in 1998. Uzbekistan also became the first recipient of a sizeable transfer of military equipment under the Foreign Military Financing program in 2000. The nature of the security threats in Uzbekistan was also slightly different from Kazakhstan, however, as the US was also gravely concerned with the mounting power of an Islamic extremist network based in Uzbekistan. And although the US also reached a CTR agreement with Uzbekistan based on the Kazakh CTR, the immediate threat was from the mounting Islamic insurgency in the country

Officially, US policy was even more ambitious, with longer-term goals of democratization and marketization, a consolidation of regional security and cooperation, and an open and unfettered environment to allow the development of the regional energy resources. This last goal effectively translated into an effort to bolster the territorial integrity and security of the Central Asian states mainly as a counterweight to Russian interference or manipulation.

By 1999, the US Congress expanded a commitment to military engagement with Central Asia, to support the economic and political independence of both Central Asia and the Southern Caucasus. There was an important stress on military-to-military cooperation, both to Westernize and professionalize the regional militaries but also to entrench the US presence in this increasingly important region. The Congress also articulated a desire for greater regional integration and cooperation, with assistance in border control and security to combat drug trafficking, nonproliferation and other transnational criminal activities. Counter-insurgency and rudimentary counter-terrorism emerged as key focal points in the wake of armed incursions by elements of the Islamic Movement of Uzbekistan (IMU) into Kyrgyzstan in the summer of 1999.

In line with containing these security threats, the US formulated an extensive new Central Asian Border Security Initiative (CASI) in April 2000, with $3 million in additional security assistance to each of the five Central Asian states. As the IMU's military operations escalated in Uzbekistan in August 2000, with several Americans even taken hostage, the State Department formally added the IMU organization to the official US roster of foreign terrorist groups. The IMU was also linked to the Al-Qaeda network of bin Laden in September 2000, adding an even greater significance to the regional security effort.

As US engagement rapidly extended throughout the Central Asian region, the importance of stability in Tajikistan and its vulnerability to the nearby Islamic militancy also led to a new US focus. With a symbolic visit to the country in May 2001, the then head of the US Central Command (CENTCOM), General Tommy Franks, recognized Tajikistan as 'a strategically important country' and pledged US security assistance.[1] The Tajiks were then successfully persuaded to follow their Central Asian neighbors into membership in NATO's PfP.

CENTRAL ASIA AND THE NATO PARTNERSHIP FOR PEACE PROGRAM (PFP)

As stated earlier, the NATO PfP served as a key channel for US (and Western) military engagement in Central Asia. Through the PfP, the newly-independent, yet still vulnerable, Central Asian nations were able to gain significant experience and contacts with the US military establishment. For the US and NATO, the program also offered a unique avenue toward fostering a greater integration of these states with Western political and military institutions. Central Asian involvement also promoted important civil-military reforms designed to enhance internal stability and democratization, and served to generally institutionalize relations with the US. A significant byproduct of this effort was its inherent deterrence of influence or interference from the potentially threatening regional powers of China, Iran and Russia.

As early as 1993, a number of military officers and civilian officials from Central Asia participated in training sessions of the George C. Marshall Center in Garmisch, Germany, and the contacts and experience derived from the broadening military-to-military programs began to lay a foundation for the modernization of the countries' fledgling armed forces. This investment was also important in initiating a concerted effort to overcome the legacy of decades of outdated and inappropriate Soviet military indoctrination and training. For the first time, the national Central Asian militaries were able to begin the formulation and development of their own national military doctrines, based on their unique national security needs rather than on external imposed Soviet determinants.[2]

Participation in the NATO PfP's multinational military exercises also played an important role in fostering greater regional cooperation and reintegration. The program's exercises provide crucial training in peacekeeping activities and develop interoperability, both of which were seriously absent in these countries. In August 1995, forces from Kyrgyzstan and Uzbekistan participated in Fort Polk's Operation 'Nugget' exercises in peacekeeping tactics for land forces, and were later joined by a Kazakh contingent in a follow-up round in July 1997. Forces from each of the three Central Asian states also completed an international amphibious exercise in North Carolina, along with forces from Canada, the Netherlands and 16 other PfP member nations. Kyrgyzstan and Kazakhstan also joined with the US and other NATO and PfP countries in March 2001 for exercises in Nova Scotia.

In addition to such out-of-area training, the armed forces from Kazakhstan, Kyrgyzstan and Uzbekistan formed a new joint peace-keeping unit in December 1995. This new unit, Centrazbat, was empowered to promote stability in the region and enable the three member-states to share tactical information and experience in peacekeeping and limited security patrol maneuvers. Multinational exercises centering on this Centrazbat unit have been held annually with forces from the US and NATO member-states providing field and command training.

Much of the burden of training and interacting with the Central Asian militaries fell to the US Special Forces.[3] The development of the Special Forces was a natural and necessary product of the recognition of a new nature of military threat coming from unconventional, irregular and often covert, insurgent or terrorist groups. The Special Forces are composed of small, purpose-designed units tasked with a wide variety of missions and roles. These highly-trained specialized units are able to assume a number of highly-focused missions quite beyond the ordinary capabilities of the more conventional, general-purpose units.

Training Central Asian units was, therefore, an appropriate assignment and best utilized the specific talents and skills of the Special Operations Forces (SOF). Such training missions, officially known as Foreign Internal Defense (FID), have long been a standard SOF assignment. The very nature of the US Special Forces as an unconventional and highly specialized adaptive force makes them suitable for training an infant military to counter threats of insurgency and terrorism.

Over the longer-term, such interaction also promotes two pillars of US foreign policy objectives: democracy and the protection of human rights. As reflected in the very motto of the Special Forces, *De Oppresso Liber* (To Free the Oppressed), the Special Forces exude a model of military honor and professionalism that is sorely lacking in these infant former Soviet states. Fortunately, the SOF were well-positioned and experienced in Central Asia even before the region would take on an abrupt and drastic strategic importance for the US after September 11, 2001.

POST-SEPTEMBER 11

The fundamental shift in the geopolitical landscape in the aftermath of September 11 cannot be stressed enough, as it abruptly recast and reordered US strategic priorities in nearly all respects. This shift is marked by a new US focus on regions and states that were traditionally regulated to the periphery of US strategy but that have now emerged as 'partners' or 'players' in the overarching US global war on terrorism campaign.

Such regions and nations are roughly split within these two camps: 'partners' or 'players'. These states and, more broadly, these regions, are seen from Washington as either being partners in a cooperative effort to help in the US campaign against terrorism or as players to be either pressured or coerced into a more compliant role in the campaign. It is in this sense that Pakistan, for example, has emerged as a 'partner', endowed with enhanced strategic importance and greater tactical utility for the US. Saudi Arabia, as a contrary example, is now seen as a 'player', with significantly less strategic clout or even reliability, and no longer a 'partner'.

These regions and, more specifically, their constituent states are also now viewed through this partner-or-player prism. In terms of US security policy, the traditionally marginal states of East and West Africa, for one glaring example, are now essential to the US counter-terrorism effort against the Al-Qaeda networks of Kenya and Djibouti, and the network's penetration of the diamond markets of Sierra Leone. Even 'failed' or 'failing' states in generally conflict-prone regions are now enjoying US attention of a grand scale.

The new security environments in Central Asia and the Southern Caucasus also demonstrate this shift in US security policy, although both have different aspects and issues for US strategy. Both regions also offer the US important roles as platforms for power projection, from Central Asia into Afghanistan and, at least potentially, from the Caucasus into the northern Middle East (most notably into Iran). But it was Central Asia that benefited most, and first, from the shift in US security. Uzbekistan, and to a lesser degree Kyrgyzstan, Tajikistan and Kazakhstan abruptly emerged as key frontline partners in the US war on terrorism and served as crucial platforms for Operation 'Enduring Freedom', the combat operations targeting the Taliban and the Al-Qaeda network in Afghanistan.

The Central Asian role in Operation 'Enduring Freedom' was both broad and extensive, with forward basing in Uzbekistan, Kyrgyzstan and Tajikistan, unfettered access to airspace and the use of bases in Kazakhstan and Turkmenistan. Kyrgyzstan, Kazakhstan and Turkmenistan also allowed more limited access by coalition aircraft. Most significantly, Uzbekistan provided the full use of its airbase at Karshi Khanabad and Tajikistan consented to the use of its air space and territory to the US military, but was subsequently pressured by Russian coercion to tone down its logistical support. The Tajiks still provided the use of Dushanbe airport, albeit on a contingency basis.

Russian pressure on Tajikistan is still potent, with the presence of roughly 7,000 troops from Russia's 201st division and an additional 11,000 Russian border guards stationed in the country. By November 2001, however, Tajikistan agreed to negotiate the US utilization of three additional airbases, at Khujand, Kurgan-Tyube and Kulyab. Kulyab was the best-equipped of the three. US access to these airbases in southern Tajikistan was significant for the establishment of a land bridge into northern Afghanistan, as well as the obvious benefit of providing for additional sorties as missions would be only an hour from their target lists.

It was the role of Uzbekistan, however, as the country with, comparatively, the most capable and advanced military in the region, that was most significant. The US and Uzbekistan concluded an agreement to expand military-to-military cooperation through joint seminars, training and partnerships with US units. This also provided the Uzbeks with an important external guarantee of security and, internally, endowed their military with much greater potential for combating and eventually defeating the Islamic extremist groups.

Kyrgyzstan was also an important partner in the region and provided the US with full basing rights in December 2001. The Kyrgyz formerly entered into a new one-year basing access agreement granting the US full use of its Manas airport. With the addition of other coalition forces during the operations, the Manas facility served as the operational base for over 3,000 foreign forces.

US AND RUSSIAN INTERESTS: CONVERGING OR CLASHING?

Equally serious and perhaps an even more immediate threat, is the potential for a clash between the competing interests of Russia and the US in the region. Although this is tempered somewhat by the overarching US-Russian strategic partnership, Russian interests in the region and its continuing geopolitical ambition to maintain dominance in Central Asia present their own set of security challenges to the US role in the region.

This potential clash of interests was demonstrated in late 2002, with the Russian Air Force's deployment of aircraft to the Kant airbase in Kyrgyzstan. The purpose of the deployment was ostensibly not to create a Russian base in Kyrgyzstan, but to develop a joint Russian-Kyrgyz military operational airbase to support the multinational Collective Rapid Deployment Forces (CRDF), established under the Collective Security Treaty (CST) and comprising one battalion from each CRDF member-state – Russia, Kazakhstan, Kyrgyzstan and Tajikistan.[4]

CENTRAL ASIA: THE THREAT OF ISLAMIC INSURGENCY

The threat to Central Asian security from the region's active and violent insurgent Islamic extremist groups has undergone a significant change since the overthrow of the Taliban and the reconstitution of a new Afghanistan. Recent attention to this security threat has shifted from a priority focus on the Islamic Movement of Uzbekistan (IMU), officially linked to the Al-Qaeda network, to the Hizb-ut-Tahrir (HT).

Much of this new focus on the HT came after the demise of the Taliban regime in Afghanistan effectively ended the IMU's role as the dominant threat. The collapse of the IMU was also speeded by a gradual erosion of its ability to utilize logistical and operational bases in Tajikistan from 1997 to 2001. The IMU actually relocated to the Taliban Afghanistan, changing its name to the Islamic Party of Turkestan (IPT) and voluntarily assuming a subservient role to the Taliban. The US victory over the Taliban, therefore, soundly defeated the IMU (or IPT) as well.

Although the end of the IMU removed a decade-long threat to regional security, the continued weakness of the Central Asian states, both in terms of limited capacities for sufficient border and even territorial control by the police and military, still fosters a security vacuum that may allow other like-minded Islamic extremist groups to emerge. This security vacuum is also exacerbated by continued security deficiencies in Afghanistan, by rising anti-Americanism in Pakistan and the potential for greater support among the disenfranchised populations of the impoverished Central Asian states. This may also be encouraged by the US military, offering new targets of opportunity for these groups.

A related challenge is the perception, both real and exaggerated, of US support for the generally repressive and autocratic Central Asian regimes. And with a focus on policies interpreted as being driven by obligations to reward the Central Asian states for their cooperation and by incentives aimed at ensuring continued security collaboration, there is a general feeling that the US has mislaid its earlier agenda of economic and political reform. This is further exacerbated by the deepening socioeconomic disparities and mounting poverty in the region, as well as by the dominance of small, corrupt clan-based elites. It is also these very same elites that usually constitute the overwhelming majority of contacts with the West, and that tend to monopolize military-to-military cooperation.

THE HIZB-UT-TAHRIR (HT)

The Hizb-ut-Tahrir (HT) exploited the overall focus on the IMU and used the inattention on its own activities to garner influence in many parts of the region throughout the 1990s. Unlike the IMU, the HT initiated a fairly impressive campaign of recruiting and influence-building based on a self-espoused 'non-violent' approach, focusing more on securing grassroots support by exploiting widespread unemployment, economic disparity and political alienation. This approach also marks the distinction between its London-based spokespersons' public platform of radical anti-Western (and rabid anti-America) rhetoric with its local approach stressing indigenous needs and concerns. This distinction also allows the HT to identify with the impoverished local population on a much deeper level than any pan-Islamic or anti-Western agenda could ever accomplish. This is most clearly evident in the HT's local tactics of articulating such local concerns as the dangers of drug trafficking, prostitution and HIV/AIDS, poverty and official corruption.

This localized strategy in the region also exploits the vulnerabilities of the Central Asian states. Specifically, the HT has become entrenched in two key areas: the political and religious. The HT has effectively exploited widespread alienation among a seriously disenfranchised and polarized population to present itself as the only true grassroots or populist organization seeking to represent (and advocate) the interests of the general population. In this regard, the HT portrays itself as a movement for economic and political justice, albeit stemming from an underlying Islamic foundation.

It has also significantly exploited the rather undeveloped nature of Islam in the region. With an already mounting hunger for information and exposure to Islam and Islamic traditions in the early years of the post-Soviet period, the HT was able to quickly offer religious instruction and non-threatening indoctrination. By establishing a network of informal Islamic teaching and semi-education, the HT emerged as the popular source for religious instruction. And by avoiding the more expensive (and more public) institutionalization of Islamic teaching through *madrasas*, for example, the HT soon acquired a virtual monopoly on religion and matters of faith in the region. This also meant that they became the providers of preference for pseudo-civil duties, offering Islamic marriages, divorce and even informal family court services.

Given the rise in poplar support and increasing authority of the HT organization, the secular governments of Central Asia recognize the HT as a serious threat to their rule and are now urging the US to label the group as a terrorist organization (following the German decision to outlaw the group). Although most analysts have warned of the dangers of such a move, contending that an identification of the group as 'terrorist' would only radicalize an already popular

grassroots organization, driving it underground and perhaps provoking a violent reaction, others argue against this self-fulfilling
prophecy argument and stress the threat posed by the HT to the
regimes of the region, although usually downplaying the serious
shortcomings, widespread corruption and human rights violations of
these regimes.

Although this debate is as yet unresolved, due consideration to
more effective measures to prevent the HT from emerging as a truly
terrorist group may be more productive for US policy in the long
run. The leverage of US engagement in the region may actually
offer two new sets of tools to more soundly combat the appeal and
resort to violence by the more radical of the region's extremist
elements. Such tools would include greater pressure for democratic
reform in the autocratic states of the region, with a widening of the
nation-building programs vital to conflict-prevention.

The US may also gain from the inherent contrast with the
Russian presence in the region. Both in terms of historical legacy
and by virtue of the perception of a current Russian threat to the
region, ranging from the reasonable, a threat from the Russian
military, to the exaggerated, a threat from the sizable Russian minority population, the US stands to benefit. Additionally, the positive
approach of US Special Forces in the region, with a successful civil
affairs operation, only reinforces this contrast. In fact, the US effort
to combat drug trafficking actually expropriates one of the core
elements of the HT platform. Once this contrast is promoted, the
US presence will not be seen by the local population as much of a
contradiction to the HT. The test here would be to contain any new
rise in anti-Western rhetoric, although the rather under-developed
state of Islam in Central Asia has meant that it has not become as
inherently defensive or confrontational as in other regions.

The second set of new tools relates to the nature of US engagement. The counter-insurgency and strengthening of capacity of the
region's militaries, already well underway, can be presented as an
effort to build the infant states of the region. By focusing on capacity
building that does not automatically arm or strengthen the regimes
themselves, any potential fear or opposition to these programs by
the HT may be countered with an appeal to nationalism. Such an
appeal to national identity, whether it is Uzbek, Kazakh or Kyrgyz
pride and national feeling, is perhaps the most natural defense
against religious-inspired extremism.

And by building stronger national armies and police, the resulting improvements in border security and the rule of law may become the most effective avenue toward meeting the very goals of justice and social order espoused by the Islamic groups like the HT. In fact the debate over the nature of the HT, as agents of transition or advocates of terrorism, actually obscures the larger challenge of securing 'regions at risk'.

Thus, the real challenge to dealing with the HT and other lesser groups is in linking US security efforts to the important social and political needs of each of the Central Asian states. Central to this challenge, as recent experience in Afghanistan has revealed only too well, is the test of time: US engagement must be based on the long-term, instituting sustainable policies to promote national and regional stability. Any abrupt departure or withdrawal from these regions would seriously impede the US engagement and may result in the 'blowback' that emerged in Afghanistan in the wake of the Soviet retreat. This lesson also confirms the dangers posed by the 'failed' and 'failing' states that are now so prominent on the US national security agenda. And with no real national capacity or regional security organizations able to assume the mantle of security and stability, the US has firmly entered a region necessitating longer-term stamina and endurance.

US ENGAGEMENT IN THE CAUCASUS

As already demonstrated, the US war on terrorism also resulted in a number of modifications in US security policy toward a number of nations. These modifications in policy affected a wide-ranging set of diverse and often disparate nations, including traditional foes of China and Russia, traditional allies and new partners. Following the development of new partners in Central Asia, the US also broadened it role in the former Soviet Union to the other side of the Caspian Sea. Although generally engaged in the region since its emergence following the fall of the Soviet Union, the three nations of the Southern Caucasus acquired a new security perspective in the wake of September 11.

Although there was also a role for the smaller Southern Caucasus states, their active contribution to the effort was far less important than the Central Asian states and consisted primarily of limited counter-terrorism training, through 'train and equip' missions in

Georgia, and greater military assistance for border security and counter-proliferation in Azerbaijan. Armenia was virtually excluded from any significant role by virtue of its continued reliance on its strategic security relationship with Russia. This Armenian reliance on Russia borders on outright dependence, however, and has contributed to a gradual upset of the traditional balance of Armenian 'complementarity' policy of balancing a pro-Western orientation with its security ties to Russia.

With the shifts in US security policies, there was also a dramatic change in the US relationship with Azerbaijan. Although the US extended some $3 million in funding for nonproliferation, anti-terrorism, de-mining and related programs (NADR) in FY2001, the US was long precluded from official military assistance by US legislation that prohibited any American aid to Azerbaijan (with the exception of funds for disarmament programs) until it demonstrated real steps to end its blockades of Armenia and the Armenian Nagorno-Karabakh enclave and the use of force against Nagorno Karabagh.

This legislation, more commonly known as Section 907 of the Freedom Support Act, was amended after September 11 to allow for a presidential waiver. After that weakening of the restrictions on aid, the Bush administration then requested $50 million for Azerbaijan in FY2002 and $52.98 million in FY2003, including $3 million in foreign military financing (FMF), $750,000 in International Military Education and Training (IMET) and $46 million in Freedom Support Act (FSA) funding.

The Azerbaijani government offered use of its airbases for coalition refueling en route to Central Asia in October 2001. By March 2001, Azerbaijan entered into the country's first security agreement with the US, calling for the US provision of specific technical assistance in air traffic control and safety, military and peace-keeping training, enhanced naval border security, and the upgrade and modernization of military airports.

THE GEORGIAN TRAIN & EQUIP PROGRAM (GTEP)

The US announced a new $64 million program of military assistance in the Southern Caucasus in March 2002 with the Georgian Train & Equip Program (GTEP), providing specialized counter-terrorism training for 2,000 elite Georgian troops. The GTEP is actually an expansion of an already active US role in bolstering security in this conflict-prone country. This effort follows such earlier involvement but represents a much more public and symbolic program, timed with continuing instability and vulnerability in Georgia. It was further designed to counter an escalation of Russian pressure at the time, mainly articulated through Moscow's threats to intervene militarily in Georgia in pursuit of Chechen rebel forces reportedly enjoying refuge in Georgia's volatile Pankisi Gorge.[5]

The core mission of the GTEP is its capacity-building role, with specialized assistance and tactical training to enhance the counterterrorism capabilities of the best of the Georgian armed forces. Theoretically, the program has two aspects: counter-terrorism, comprising offensive measures, and anti-terrorism, with defensive measures. The GTEP serves as a component in the other US counter-terrorism efforts underway in a number of countries and aims to bolster stability in the Southern Caucasus.

The program also shares some similarities with the training and equipping of Colombian military forces involved in counter-insurgency and counter-drug operations. A shared goal of both the Colombian and Georgian Train & Equip programs is to assist the local government to 'regain control over its national territory' but by maintaining a firm line against having US forces deploy in any combat operations. The program in Colombia also parallels the Georgian effort in the need to bolster a beleaguered state under threat by insurgencies, as both states are beset by undermined sovereignty.

In Colombia the threat is posed by the rebel FARC and ELN movements, both of which are closely linked to narco-trafficking, while in the Georgian case, the threat is from the breakaway, self-declared independent 'republics' of Abkhazia and South Ossetia. And although there is no drug production in Georgia (although it is a major issue in Central Asia), there is a growing danger of proliferation and conflict spillover from nearby Chechnya. Through innovative 'train-the-trainer' efforts, US SOF serve as an important, and most times as the only, force to professionalize and modernize the local armed forces, introducing a new respect for human rights and a commitment to banish war crimes and ethnic cleansing from such conflict-prone regions.

Designed as a flexible, time-phased training initiative, the GTEP supplements the bilateral military-to-military relationship already well developed over the past nearly 14 years. The program is not designed to provide the Georgian military with any offensive capabilities that would upset the region's rather delicate balance of power, however, and is much more inwardly focused. Moreover, the training and equipment provided by the US is much less a broad effort to endow Georgia with a combat-ready fighting force, but is much more a rather limited and symbolically important demonstration of the US commitment and support for Georgian sovereignty, independence and territorial integrity.

The initial GTEP program, launched in May 2002, consisted of command center staff training for members of the Georgian Ministry of Defense as well as staff training for units of the Land Forces Command by select members of the US Army Special Forces assigned to Special Operations Command, Europe (SOCEUR). Some elements of the Border Guards and other Georgian security agencies were added later to ensure interoperability among the Georgian security forces. But elements of the Georgian National Guard were explicitly excluded from the program due to their ties to paramilitary militia groups operating during the country's devastating civil war in the early to mid-1990s.

The overall goal is to forge strong and effective staff organizations capable of creating and sustaining standardized operating procedures, training and operational plans, and able to administer an open and accountable defense property management system. The curriculum consists of performance-oriented training and practical exercises based on the National Defense University, Joint Forces Command and US Army War College models. Staff training is designed to last for roughly 70 days and is conducted in a small group or classroom setting.

In addition to staff training, tactical training is provided sequentially, consisting of approximately 100 days per unit. The goal of the tactical program is to instruct Georgian battalions in light infantry tactics, including platoon-level offensive and defensive operations and basic airmobile tactics. The curriculum for the tactics training encompasses basic individual skills, such as combat lifesaver, radio operator procedures, land navigation and human rights education. It further includes individual combat skills, such as rifle marksmanship, individual movement techniques, and squad and platoon tactics.

During the course of the GTEP, the Georgian units are also provided with military equipment such as uniform items, small arms and ammunition, communications gear, training gear, medical gear, fuel and construction materiel.

GTEP TRAINING OVERVIEW

Background
The GTEP mission began in May 2002 with US Army Special Forces assigned to Special Operations Command, Europe (SOCEUR)

Phase I
Logistics/Engineering

Phase IIA and IIB
Military Joint Doctrine, Command and Control, Staff/ Organizational Training for the Georgian Ministry of Defense and Land Forces Command

Phase IIIA
Unit level tactical training of the Georgian Commando Battalion

Phase IIIB
Unit level tactical training and specialized military mountain-eering training for the 16th Mountain Battalion

GTEP Mission
To enhance the capability of selected Georgian military units to provide security and stability to the citizens of Georgia and the region

A flexible, time-phased training initiative

Phase IIIC Light Infantry Battalion
Goal: To train the 560-man 113th Light Infantry Battalion/ 11th Motorized Riffle Brigade to conduct patrol base operations, ambush procedures, urban terrain operations, long-range patrols, platoon-level raids, and daylight company-level attacks and night defensive operations

Length of training – 100-day period of instruction

Task Force GTEP is comprised of elements from the US Marine Corps (USMC), US Army, US Air Force (USAF) and US Navy

The US Marine Corps assumed direct control of the GTEP mission in December 2002 and was commanded by Marine Corps Major Scott Campbell.[6] The Task Force GTEP is a joint mission but utilizes Marine instructors and trainers who provide command and control of the program and are experts in their Military Occupational Specialties of Infantry Small Unit Tactics, Marine Corps marksmanship and infantry battalion weapons systems.

Additionally, the Army provides a Forward Surgical Team and a detachment from its 7th Signal Brigade for long-haul communications, as well as providing communication and first aid classes to the soldiers. The Air Force serves as the contracting party for the GTEP program and is the liaison between the program and private contractors. The Navy recently became a part of the GTEP mission by taking over the job of providing mail services.

The GTEP involves training a total of four battalion-sized elements during the entire training evolution, with each battalion receiving instruction in a specific area of training. The first battalion receives instruction in mountain warfare operations, the second and third battalions in light infantry operations, and the fourth battalion is given training in mechanized warfare. Each battalion is similar to a Marine Corps rifle battalion and is comprised of three rifle companies, a headquarters company, and consists of about 560 personnel. A common factor to all of the battalions is that they have recently been created and have not received substantial infantry training.

Prior to even reaching the training range, the Georgian soldiers participating in the program must first begin their training with 'Zero' week. The soldiers must pass a physical fitness test, are issued their uniforms and weapon and are then given a complete eye exam. Throughout the 14-week training cycle, the three line companies of the battalion and its Head Quarters and Service (H&S) Company work in a round-robin type format.

During the first four weeks of training, each company focuses on infantry tactics, land navigation, first aid, and fire and movement. The H&S company receives specialized training for each staff section and the supporting platoons. In weeks five through seven, the soldiers begin work on their marksmanship and move into squad tactical training and patrol operations. They also work on fire team and squad rushes and illuminated night attack scenarios.

Platoon Tactical Training begins in week eight and continues through week ten with formations and immediate action drills, ambushes, patrol base operations and supported attacks in the offense. The soldiers begin Military Operations in Urban Terrain in weeks 11 through 13. Offensive and defensive combat tactics, raids and "Movement to Contact" are also a focus during this period of instruction. Week 14 is the culmination point of the training for the Georgian soldiers. Each company is required to conduct a challenging daylight live-fire supported attack, combining everything the soldiers have learned to this point. Machine guns, AK-47s and RPGs are used in conjunction with other weapons systems to reach the final objective and test the skills of not only the company officers and non-commissioned officers (NCOs), but every Georgian soldier involved.

The Phase IIIC portion of the program was launched in May 2003. This portion provides training for the 560-man Georgian 113th Light Infantry Battalion/11th Motorized Rifle Brigade in patrol base operations, ambush procedures, urban terrain operations, long-range patrols, platoon-level raids, daylight company-level attacks and night defensive operations.

Following the completion of Phase IIIC, the Marine staff proceeded to initiate the next phases of the program, Phase IIID, Light Infantry Battalion, and Phase IIIE, Mechanized Company Team, through the scheduled end of the program in May 2004. The Georgian participants in the Train an& Equip Program receive diverse training focused on skills that all infantry soldiers require to be competent in the combat environment, including land mine warfare, claymore anti-personnel mine employment and live-fire hand grenade practical application. As part of the curriculum, the soldiers learn the basics of each subject, to include detecting land mines, marking and reporting minefields, setting up claymore mines and proper techniques of throwing hand grenades.

During the land mine warfare classes, the soldiers are taught the nomenclature of a mine and the components of a mine. They are also taught the types of mines, to include anti-tank and anti-personnel, and to detect, mark and report mines and minefields.

Claymore mine classes are given with the emphasis being placed on the claymore being utilized as a key weapon to be employed in an ambush, defense position or used to provide anti-personnel capabilities for patrol base defense. GTEP training also covers hand grenades (used for close-in fighting, trench and building clearing and urban warfare) and smoke grenades (used for marking and obscuring the battlefield).

Communications training is also an important element in the GTEP, with a one-day basic communications class beginning in the third week of the 14-week training cycle. Georgian soldiers begin with hands-on instruction in the lightweight Harris radio system, learning to send and receive radio messages and the proper use of a call sign. Classes on frequencies and transmitters and receivers are also introduced.

An additional five-day advanced communications training program is offered to the communications platoon, the scouts and reconnaissance section and many of the squad team and fire team leaders. In this part of the program, out of the 558 soldiers that receive basic communications training, only 85 are selected to move on to the advanced communications program, however.

Advanced communication skills include antenna propagation and field antennas, radio waves and terrain analysis and masking. Also included is the coordinating, setting up and running of a sub-station – utilized at the squad, company and battalion levels, and a net control station – utilized at the company and battalion levels. The final step in the advanced communications training program is bringing the entire skill-set together to run a company radio room and combat operations center radio room.

Another essential training feature is land navigation. Although many of the participants are conscripts with little or no military experience, there are some challenges for the Marine instructors with some of the officers and NCOs in ensuring that they overcome their prior training in Soviet-style land navigation, more used to Soviet maps and compasses. This one-week portion of the training is designed to both teach new soldiers and to provide Western or NATO standards for those with Soviet military backgrounds. Specifically, the training focuses on land navigation and cover and concealment, with the soldiers learning to navigate through the training environment by using a 1:50,000 topographical map, a protractor and a lensatic compass.

The students are also taught to find an azimuth, determine direction, change grid to magnetic angle and perform a resection using the map and compass method. Practical application is done in the field and soldiers are challenged by both a day and night course, and are expected to pass the course as individuals in the day course and as teams at night. Cover and concealment instruction also begins in the classroom with emphasis being placed on camouflage and target identification, including movement, sound and noise discipline. During the practical application phase of the training, the soldiers are given additional instruction on applying camouflage paint with emphasis on proper and improper camouflage techniques.

Despite the obvious merits of the GTEP, the overall outlook for Georgia is troubling. Georgia is now in danger of entering a final, and possibly fatal, stage as a 'failed state'. The realignment of Russian and US interests in combating terrorism implies a more accepting view of Russian actions in Chechnya and suggests a renewed Russian determination to maintain influence over Georgia. It also seems likely that Russian cooperation in the US anti-terror campaign will result in increased Russian pressure on the Shevardnadze government to adopt stronger measures to combat the presence of Chechen rebel bases and supply lines within Georgian territory. The Chechen threat from Georgia, both real and exaggerated, will continue to be used to justify a halt to the withdrawal of Russian forces from their remaining bases in Georgia and will be used as political leverage over the weakened Georgian government.

But the main obstacle presently facing the US engagement in Georgia does not necessarily come solely from a confrontation with Russia, but is posed by the reality of Georgia's internal vulnerability. No matter how successful US-Georgian operations are in securing the Pankisi Gorge and no matter how effective US training is in reforming the Georgian armed forces, the overall objectives of enhancing stability and sovereignty are bound to be constrained by the fundamental vulnerability of the Georgian state.

By seeking security over longer-term strategy, the military focus will do little to bridge the divide between the central Georgian government and the separatist movements in the breakaway republics of Abkhazia and South Ossetia and will most likely foster greater tension in the other regions of Ajaria and Javakheti. The only viable hope for the Republic of Georgia lies in recasting the country into a new confederation/federation. But with little or no promise for real political stability, the path to this new Georgia remains seriously hindered by a number of internal deficiencies and weakness.

The lack of an overall strategy addressing the fundamental problems of rampant corruption and internal political discord suggests that the decline of Georgia will only be temporarily arrested at best. This situation also presents a danger, however, as Georgia is the only country where a Russian, Turkish and US military presence all converge.

CONSTRAINTS AND CONSIDERATIONS

While generally the performance of US military forces in the global war on terrorism to date has been impressive, there are some troubling factors indicating a more difficult period in the next phase or next theater in this campaign. The transformation of the US military sought by the Bush administration and directed by Defense Secretary Donald Rumsfeld tends to favor the operational needs of the US engagement in Central Asia and the Southern Caucasus. The stress on a future force defined less by size and more by mobility and swiftness, and that is easier to deploy and sustain, complements the force structure and operational characteristics of the US effort in Central Asia and the Southern Caucasus. Much of this transformation is driven by the three primary risk areas set forth in the 2001 Quadrennial Defense Review (QDR): force management, operational and institutional risk.

The abrupt September 11 shift in security, as well as the subsequent campaigns in Afghanistan and Iraq, have only reinforced this effort and led to a new priority, in both policy and funding, for addressing asymmetric threats and for the SOF that are best poised to meet this threat. The SOF are now positioned with an enhanced role that, according to new Assistant Secretary of Defense for Special Operations and Low Intensity Conflict Thomas O'Connell, given its 'unique capability to meet the complex new challenges of the global war on terrorism has increased their importance as a primary tool in the nation's defense – as opposed to merely a tool for leveraging conventional forces or for smaller, specialized mission'.[7]

SOF is in the best position to meet the changing nature of threats due to its transformational nature and by virtue of its specific core tasks. The SOF are organized, trained and equipped to specifically accomplish nine core tasks:

1. Counter-Proliferation (CP);
2. Combating Terrorism (CBT);
3. Foreign Internal Defense (FID);
4. Special Reconnaissance (SR);
5. Direct Action (DA);

6. Psychological Operations (PSYOP);
7. Civil Affairs Operations (CA);
8. Unconventional Warfare (UW); and
9. Information Operations (IO).

Aside from these nine core tasks, however, SOF also increasingly face newer activities: coalition support, counter-narco-terrorism, foreign humanitarian assistance, combat search and rescue, humanitarian de-mining operations and security/peace operations. SOF are also adept in managing the transformation of theaters from one of military action and combat, to one of stabilization and low- intensity conflict, and then eventually on to local civilian control and the reestablishment of security. Such adaptation is applicable to both the Central Asian and Southern Caucasus theaters, as both regions are currently attempting to transition from conflict to post-conflict security environments.

Additionally, an added organization change has elevated the SOF by 'retooling' the US Special Operations Command (USSOCOM) to no longer serve primarily as a supporting command, but to enable it to plan and execute key missions as a supported combatant command. This upgrade in status further allows USSOCOM to expand its combat missions 'directly against terrorist organizations around the world, while maintaining its role of force provider and supporter to the geographic combatant commanders'.[8]

Another factor contributing to the enhanced role for SOF is the modified concept of stability operation that, as in Afghanistan and Iraq, has demonstrated a 'transition of theater from one of military action, to one of stabilization and low-intensity conflict, and then eventually on to local civilian control, is difficult and benefits form the specific skills and capabilities of SOF, especially Civil Affairs and Psychological Operations forces'.[9] The USSOCOM is also transforming SOF capabilities by enhancing sustained operations in target areas and investing in 'low density/high demand' aviation assets for SOF use.

Much of this focus on special operations to meet the asymmetric, unconventional threats, often emanating form non-state actors, has been bolstered by the impressive performance of the SOF force deployed in Operation 'Enduring Freedom' (and throughout Operation 'Iraqi Freedom'). In that Afghanistan campaign, a force of less than 500 SOF personnel mounted an interagency and combined unconventional warfare effort, tied closely to indigenous forces and linked the US Air Force that achieved a rapid defeat of the Taliban's conventional forces. This operation was executed by small units operating with autonomy in a highly fluid environment and prosecuted by SOF personnel able to join with friendly Afghan forces and able to function effectively within five key parameters:

- operate effectively without a 'safety net';
- develop a firm rapport and trust with Afghan allies;
- operate without any significant logistics train to provide equipment and supplies;
- distinguish between combatants and non-combatants in a difficult and confused environment (civilians and combatants, Taliban and non-Taliban, and ex-Taliban all mixed together in a compact area);
- engineer combined arms operations between US Air Force assets (B-52s) and Northern Alliance armored units (Soviet-era tanks).

Special Operations personnel also performed well in Operation 'Iraqi Freedom', as USSOCOM provided 7,270 Special Operations personnel and 152 Special Operations-skilled reservists (individual augmentees) to support two Combined Joint Special Operations Task Forces established by Special Operations Command-Central Command in the area of operations. Some of the key 'lessons learned' from Iraq involved special operations training and doctrine, early deployment of special operations and joint force integration. The engagement of special operations in advance of combat operations proved successful and was a major contributing factor for successful operations in Northern Iraq. In terms of joint force integration, there were several cases of conventional units under the operational control (OPCON) of SOF commanders, and SOF units OPCON of conventional commanders.[10]

This applicability of the particular skill sets of SOF personnel to the needs and challenges unique to the Central Asian and Southern Caucasus regions is one of the most essential elements in the US engagement in these regions. These SOF skill sets include unique training and specialization, extensive overseas experience and language abilities (as well as cultural and religious awareness), the ability to work with and train indigenous forces, and the capability to 'blend' into the fabric of the host society in which SOF personnel operate. These human assets are ideally tailored to the US effort in the tradition-based and heritage-rich Central Asian and Southern Caucasus states.

LESSONS LEARNED: SPECIAL OPERATIONS IN AFGHANISTAN AND IRAQ

The preliminary (and casual) 'lessons learned' from the SOF operations in Operation 'Enduring Freedom' and Operation 'Iraqi Freedom' reveal proven flexibility, innovation 'on the fly' and improved methods that enhanced the effectiveness of highly sophisticated long-range weapons, all with a very small 'footprint'. This performance contributes to the utilization of the SOF as 'critical incubators' for methods, techniques and equipment to enhance combat effectiveness. Training is also a key contributor to overall readiness and specialization and follows the SOF commitment to 'train for certainty, educate for uncertainty'. The SOF training regime is intense, extensive and specialized, with four critical elements:

Realistic combat training. This includes realistic and live-fire training with an adequate integration of modern weapons and techniques on a large scale, involving land, sea and air assets. Urban combat training facilities are increasingly important, as is the occasional but important use of infrastructural facilities, such as nuclear power plants and major seaport facilities.

Adequate mission planning and rehearsal. Systems providing the ability to integrate real-time information into operations planning and full rehearsal provide virtual 'eyes-on-target' that enhances operational success.

Global access and exposure. This is comprised of Joint Combined Exchange Training (JCETs), humanitarian de-mining programs and counter-drug cooperation. Language training is also essential in this training module.

Selection and standards. The selection and standards of SOF personnel is perhaps the most important element in understanding SOF's unique skills and versatility. Standards must withstand the pressures for increased operation tempo and be able to maintain high quality over the need for quantity.

Cutting edge technology is also an important supplement to training and is essential to maintain the SOF's competitive advantage in the face of evolving threats. Most modern terrorist groups today, for example, are able to easily acquire sophisticated secure wireless communications, global positioning systems (GPS), night vision gear and other tools that were solely available to military forces only a few years ago. Therefore, the constant effort to keep pace with, and actually surpass, the commercial market for such equipment is a crucial component in proper SOF acquisition and development.

THE DANGERS: ESCALATING OPTEMPO AND OVEREXTENSION

The dangers, however, stem from two troubling trends: an upsurge in operational tempo (OPTEMPO) and an ever-increasing rate of deployment and demand, with broadened involvement in humanitarian and peacekeeping missions.[11] The SOF accounts for a mere 1.4 per cent of the total force structure and traditionally only about 3.6 per cent of the overall Department of Defense (DoD) budget. Yet the increase in OPTEMPO for the SOF is dramatic: In 1993, USSOCOM averaged 2,036 personnel deployed away from their home station each week, serving in about 101 countries; by 1996, the number of personnel climbed to 4,613, and by 1999, to 5,141, deployed in 149 countries and foreign territories. And that pre-September 11 OPTEMPO has only naturally expanded in the past thee years.

Both factors are fundamentally challenging to the overall commitment and durability of the US strategic presence in these regions. The sheer scope of global force requirements, compounded by a recent record of an opaque and even contradictory rotation plan, has placed severe pressure on morale among many active and reserve components. And the steady increase in the SOF OPTEMPO must be addressed, as both quality and quantity are firmly linked to the OPTEMPO, so much so that any imbalance in one of the three links inherently upsets the balance of the other components.

The new USSOCOM Commander, General Bryan Brown, also expressed concern over the OPTEMPO, which he cited in July 2003 as 'the highest it has ever been' for the SOF. Much to his credit, General Brown has also pledged to address this as a 'major threat to readiness' by prioritizing mission selection while stressing that 'selection, assessment, training and retention of quality people will be keys to maintaining the readiness' of the SOF.[12]

This vast global presence is also generally under-appreciated, with significant ongoing operations in Iraq, Afghanistan, the Balkans, the Horn of Africa, Colombia and other parts of South America, as well as the long-standing deployment in Korea, and not to mention a potential deployment to Liberia, only demonstrating the most overt and open US presence. Looking at the Balkans alone, SOF elements have been deployed in Bosnia-Herzegovina since 1995 and in both Kosovo and Macedonia since 1999.

Other related dangers of overextension stem from the mounting nature of needs, as in today's post-conflict Afghanistan, for example. Military planners now see a need to immediately increase the number of Provincial Reconstruction Teams (PRT) to eight, for deployment in each Afghan province. Forces are also required to expand operations underway along the Afghan-Pakistani border aimed at interdicting infiltration/exfiltration routes that Al-Qaeda and Taliban remnants are still utilizing.

A rapid acceleration of SOF training for the fledgling Afghan National Army is another priority, as the transfer of security responsibilities has been hostage to the readiness and size of the Afghan army. The Afghan National Army is to be expanded to some 7,200 by January 2004 and to 10,000 by June 2004, although even then it remains doubtful whether it will be able to effectively counter the growing influence of the disparate 'warlords' who have emerged as the local players in most regions and areas beyond the Afghani capital Kabul. These are just two burdens in only one theater of operations that present a drain on SOF resources and personnel.

The president's FY2004 budget submission calls for $1.7 billion increased funding for the SOF. Much of this increase proposes funding for fixed and rotary-wing aviation, SEAL teams, Civil Affairs (CA), Psychological Operations (PSYOP), Theater Special Operations Commands and greater support for USSOCOM as the supported combatant commander in the war on terrorism. Despite the FY2004 budget request for an increase of 2,563 SOF personnel, bringing the total end strength in FY2004 to 49,848 personnel, there is concern over the rate of attrition and declines in retention among the SOF community. There have been a few new initiatives introduced over the past year aimed at addressing problems in recruiting, training and retaining SOF personnel, although the only visible immediate effect was the option for Army recruits to sign up for Special Forces directly, rather than await selection from conventional units.

FOCUSING ON PSYOP AND CA FORCES

There has also been a recent recognition of the all-important need to strengthen and build psychological operations (PSYOP) and civil affairs (CA). The stabilization effort underway in both Afghanistan and Iraq has only too clearly highlighted the urgent need to enhance PSYOP capabilities to penetrate denied areas and to more effectively wage, and win, the 'war of ideas'. The planned increases in PSYOP active component forces include an additional two regional and one tactical PSYOP companies, with reserve components set to receive an additional four regional PSYOP companies. The USSOCOM also plans to create a 70-person Joint PSYOP Support Element to provide dedicated joint PSYOP planning expertise to the Geographic Combatant Commanders, Strategic Command and the Secretary of Defense. Beyond personnel, there is also an effort underway to modernize PSYOP equipment with a specific focus on using unmanned aerial vehicles (UAVs) and satellite technologies, for example.

For Army CA forces, a similar effort is underway to add four reserve component battalions and 84 positions to the Army's sole active duty CA battalion (the 96th).[13] An interesting side note to the CA force structure is the fact that some 97 per cent of all CA forces are drawn from reserve components. This is seen by some as an advantage, allowing the combatant commander to utilize the reservists' civilian 'real world' expertise in such crucial areas as civil administration, public safety, economics and commerce. Others, including new US Army Chief of Staff General Peter Shoomaker, see this as more of an imbalance, noting that active components, with traditional tactical skill sets, are without the civilian-acquired specialties that reside only in the reserve component.[14]

CONCLUSION

There have been a limited, but significant set of analyses produced in the past three years that provide a comprehensive review of the US military engagement in Central Asia and the Southern Caucasus. Three such reports stand out in their thorough consideration of the challenges and constraints facing the US presence in these regions.

The first report of note, 'US Military Engagement with Transcaucasia and Central Asia', was released in June 2000 for the

Strategic Studies Institute of the US Army College. This report was written by Dr Stephen Blank and offered one of the few comprehensive studies of the US 'strategy of engaging and enlarging the democratic community of states' with a focus on Transcaucasia and Central Asia as 'important testing grounds of this strategy, by virtue of their strategic location adjacent to Russia, the Middle East, and Europe's periphery, and their large-scale oil and natural gas deposits'.

The report offers an insightful pre-September 11 look at the strategic imperatives driving the US engagement in these regions at that time. Blank correctly identifies that the US engagement may lead to 'an intensifying focus of international rivalry with Russia' stemming from Moscow's recognition of these two regions as integral 'spheres of influence' and a Russian 'willingness to contest expanding US interests forcefully'. The report also warns that the US engagement in these 'sensitive' regions must 'review to what degree we are creating an implied commitment to defend these governments against both internal and external threats to their security and independence'. Blank goes on to explain that 'military engagement cannot become, as it has been, an uncontrolled version of mission creep by which training and provision of assistance becomes a policy that ties our hands and creates an atmosphere of moral commitment that may be unjustified in some crises.

Blank concludes by stressing that 'there is a great danger that in the Transcaspian, because of the importance of access to energy and of balancing the Russian presence, we are drifting into an unplanned but protracted military presence'. He notes that 'such a drift is the opposite of strategy because it represents a policy of short-run opportunism...' and reports that 'our current regional engagement represents programs that address only a relatively small but important part of the regional threats to security, but do so in an improvised fashion'. He then concludes by warning that such 'inspired improvisation is not sufficient as a policy or as a strategy'.

A second probing analysis, 'Growing US Security Interests in Central Asia', was written by Dr Elizabeth Wishnik for the US Army War College's Strategic Studies Institute in October 2002. Wishnik offers a cautionary analysis warning of several shortcomings in the US approach to the region and highlights several important potential dangers for the continued US presence in Central Asia. Specifically, she stresses that 'although anti-terrorism cooperation has dominated US security interests in Central Asia since 9/11, over the long term domestic insurgencies within these states and inter-state rivalry will pose a greater threat to the region than transnational terrorist groups such as Al-Qaeda'.

To better meet this 'greater threat', she calls for an improved US 'regional strategy' that would effectively meet 'a wide range of potential sources of regional instability, including conflicts over water resource management, border disputes, refugee issues, environmental concerns, and drug trafficking'. Wishnik further sees the current US position as facing 'a choice of two vastly different policy directions. One would involve a unilateral strategy, based on self-defense and preemptive attack against terrorist groups and regimes, while the second would support continued multilateral collaboration against transnational threats'. The author goes on to conclude that a prudent resolution of this choice is readily apparent, as

... a unilateral strategy would accentuate public suspicion of US intentions in Central Asia and erode support in Russia and China for Washington's regional anti-terrorism efforts, potentially resurrecting regional initiatives aimed at minimizing the United States role in the region. Multilateral collaboration, on the other hand, would encourage the Central Asian militaries to work with each other and within the framework of western military and political institutions. To this end, intelligence-sharing, PfP and joint peace-keeping activities should be continued and greater training for Central Asian military and security officials should be provided. In deference to regional sensitivities, the United States should recognize its outsider status in Central Asia and work within existing regional structures ...

... One of the key lessons of 9/11 is that despite its preponderant power, the United States remains vulnerable to transnational threats and requires the collaboration of other states to combat them. In Central Asia, this will require a redefinition of US security interests and development of a regional strategy that would address the interrelated nature of political, economic, and security problems in the region.

A third important and relevant study was produced by RAND's Arroyo Center. Released in 2003, RAND editors Olga Oliker and Thomas Szayna compiled several insightful analyses by various analysts that examined the current US engagement in both regions. This most recent study, 'Faultlines of Conflict in Central Asia and the South Caucasus. Implications for the US Army', provides the latest information and data to present an effective overview of the current situation and to highlight several key challenges to US strategic objectives in the regions.

Perhaps most significant is the RAND study's point that 'the key factor for the likelihood of regional conflict is the regimes themselves; their weaknesses and volatilities leave them increasingly unable to withstand challenges posed by other faultlines'. This point is shared by Fiona Hill of the Brookings Institution, who also contends that 'the stability and development of the states of Central Asia and the Caucasus are threatened by their extreme domestic fragility'.[15]

This point also illuminates the dangers posed by 'failed' and 'failing' states that, with their inherent internal instability and the collapse of effective state authority, invite a rapid multiplication of challenges to US engagement beyond the initial period of entry. Moreover, this scenario also reveals the risks inherent in the US presence in such restive areas, as the fundamental threats to these states' very sovereignty greatly complicates US objectives and may make any future US disentanglement from these weak states very costly indeed.

Another significant point in this RAND study is its analysis that 'the same factors that make conflict more likely – ethnic cleavages, economic hardship, high crime rates, rampant corruption, etc – also complicate any and all efforts, military, economic, or otherwise, in the region'. The authors also noted 'whatever the extent and form of the longer-term US presence in the region, it will therefore be challenging – and challenged' and that 'even without these problems, the terrain is difficult and distances are substantial, while infrastructure throughout the region leaves much to be desired'.

The analysis goes on to warn that 'with US troops already in place to varying extents in Central Asian and South Caucasus states, it becomes particularly important to understand the faultlines, geography, and other challenges this part of the world presents'. Also important to the authors is the fact that US forces must address these issues 'regardless of the depth of their commitment to the region' but that 'the current situation, however, suggests that they may have to face them somewhat sooner than expected'.

The Central Asian region also shares a landlocked dependency, both in terms of relying on an external guarantee of security as well as in terms of economics and energy export routes. This dependency, combined with the internal weakness of these states, contributes to the challenges facing a sustained US engagement in the region.

Yet even given this shared dependence, the outlook for the US engagement in Central Asia is generally more promising than with the case of the Caucasus. This outlook is also held by Fiona Hill who stated in September 2002 that 'the importance of regional cooperation on key issues is recognized by all state governments, and the prospects are ultimately better for cooperation in Central Asia than in the Caucasus, given the fact that the political tensions there have led to less acute conflicts'.[16]

She also noted the challenges in achieving such cooperation, however. Specifically, Hill stressed the complicated and often competing factors needed, as:

further progress in promoting cooperation rather than conflict in Central Asia and the Caucasus will thus depend on the political posture of the United States, other key donor states, and on international organizations and their ability to coordinate, themselves, in delivering assistance to regional states. It will also greatly depend on the attitudes of the regional states and their governments' commitment to and capacity for domestic reform and development.[17]

And as Fiona Hill notes, 'the US will have to stay the course and continue its economic, political, and military engagement. The development and stabilization of the fractured and fragile states of Central Asia and the Caucasus is a long-term endeavor'. Although some analysts predict a US withdrawal as inevitable, Hill correctly concludes by stressing that 'such a disengagement would undermine American credibility as well as negate the increased assistance efforts...' of recent years, adding that 'as recent experience in Afghanistan has demonstrated, the risks of disengagement are significant'.

Thus, the course of the US engagement in Central Asia and the South Caucasus faces a wide array of challenges and constraints, although it is as evident that it is far too late, and too costly, for any real consideration of a withdrawal at this stage. As the US engagement deepens, the stability and security of the region and their component states are now solidly dependent on the durability and stamina of the US commitment. One can only hope that these expectations are adequately met in the medium- to long-term, especially give the looming threats of a Russian reassertion, and a Chinese ambition, of geopolitical dominance in each strategic region.

REFERENCES

1. Blank, Stephen. 'The Future of Transcaspian Security', Strategic Studies Institute, US Army War College, Aug. 2002.
2. Blank, Stephen. 'US Military Engagement with Transcaucasia and Central Asia', Strategic Studies Institute, US Army War College, June 2000.
3. Department of Defense, 'Transformation Planning Guidance', April 2003.
4. DeTemple, James, Lt. Col., 'Military Engagement in the South Caucasus', *Joint Force Quarterly* (JFQ) (Autumn/Winter 2001–02).
5. Fairbanks, Charles, C. Richard Nelson, S. Fredrick Starr and Weisbrode, Kenneth, *Strategic Assessment of Central Eurasia*, (Washington, DC: The Atlantic Council of the United States and the Central Asia-Caucasus Institute of Johns Hopkins University, Paul H. Nitze School of Advanced International Studies 2001).
6. Fredholm, Michael, 'Uzbekistan & the Threat From Islamic Extremism', Defence Academy of the United Kingdom, Conflict Studies Research Centre, March 2003.
7. Giragosian, Richard, 'Security in the Transcaucasus', presentation to the Regional Studies Course, 24th Semi-Annual International Affairs Symposium, Special Operations Academic Facility, John F. Kennedy Special Warfare Center & School, US Army, 3rd Battalion, 1st Special Warfare Training Group (Airborne), Fort Bragg, NC, 19–21 May 2003.
8. Giragosian, Richard, 'US Foreign Policy and the War on Terrorism: Implications for the Caucasus', presentation, University of Toronto, Centre for Russian and East European Studies (CREES), Toronto, Canada, 20 March 2003.
9. Hill, Fiona, 'Areas for Future Cooperation or Conflict in Central Asia and the Caucasus', Yale University Conference, 'The Silk Road in the 21st Century', 19 Sept. 2002.
10. International Crisis Group (ICG), 'Tajikistan: A Roadmap for Development', 24 April 2003.
11. Oliker, Olga and Szayna, Thomas (eds.), 'Faultlines of Conflict in Central Asia and the South Caucasus. Implications for the US Army', RAND, Arroyo Center, 2003.
12. O'Malley, William and McDermott, Roger, 'The Russian Air Force in Kyrgyzstan: The Security Dynamics', *The Analyst*, Central Asia-Caucasus Institute, Johns Hopkins University, 9 April 2003.
13. O'Malley, William, 'Evaluating Possible Airfield Deployment Options: Middle East Contingencies', RAND, MR-1353-AF, 2001.
14. Sarafian, Gregory, 'Islamic Extremism in Former Soviet Republics', *Military Review* (May–June 2001) pp.64–70.
15. Sokolsky, Richard and Charlick-Paley, Tanya, 'NATO and Caspian Security, A Mission Too Far?', RAND, MR-1074-AF, 1999.
16. United States Senate Armed Services Committee, hearing testimony of Lt. General Bryan D. Brown as nominee for Commander, US Special Operations Command (SOCOM), 29 July 2003.
17. United States Senate Armed Services Committee, hearing testimony of Thomas W. O'Connell as nominee for Assistant Secretary of Defense for Special Operations and Low Intensity Conflict, 10 July 2003.
18. Wishnik, Elizabeth, 'Growing US Security Interests in Central Asia', Strategic Studies Institute, US Army War College, Oct. 2002.

NOTES

1. The five Central Asian states were formally transferred from the US European Command to CENTCOMM in Oct. 1999.
2. The only exception to the five Central Asian states is Tajikistan, which formed its national armed forces around the remnants of several armed groups involved in the country's civil war. All other Central Asian states reconstituted their armed forces on the inheritance of units of the Soviet Turkistan Military District.
3. The Special Forces, known officially as the US Army Special Forces and unofficially as the 'Green Berets', comprises a very small element in the overall US military known as Special Operations Forces (SOF), codified by the Nunn-Cohen Amendment to the Goldwater-Nichols Defense Reform Act of 1986.
4. William O'Malley and Roger McDermott, 'The Russian Air Force in Kyrgyzstan: The Security Dynamics', *The Analyst*, Central Asia-Caucasus Institute, Johns Hopkins University, 9 April 2003.
5. The Pankisi Gorge is a nearly 30-mile long valley of rock and forest roughly 80 miles from Tbilisi and has been beyond the control of the central Georgian government for some time, with a minimal police presence limited to the roads leading into and out of the gorge. Separated from Chechnya by 36 miles of rugged mountainous terrain, the gorge is populated by large numbers of Chechen refugees and local ethnic Chechens, but is dominated by well-armed informal paramilitary militias and criminal gangs engaged in the smuggling of arms and narcotics, exacerbated by severe unemployment and under-development.
6. As of Aug. 2003.
7. Testimony of Thomas O'Connell, Senate Armed Services Committee hearing on his nomination as Assistant Secretary of Defense for Special Operations and Low Intensity Conflict, 10 July 2003.
8. Ibid.
9. Ibid.
10. Testimony of Lieutenant General Bryan D. Brown, Senate Armed Services Committee hearing on his nomination as Commander, US Special Operations Command (USSOCOM), 29 July 2003.
11. SOF involvement in such 'Operations Other Than War' (OOTW) has steadily increased to also include disaster relief, noncombatant evacuation, humanitarian de-mining operations, public health and refugee aid, and the enforcement of sanctions or exclusionary zones.
12. Testimony of Lieutenant General Bryan D. Brown (note 10).
13. Of the four additional CA battalions, one is already 'on line' with the second to follow shortly. The two other battalions are to be activated in 2004 and 2005, respectively.
14. Testimony of Lieutenant General Peter J. Shoomaker, Senate Armed Services Committee hearing on his nomination as Chief of Staff of the US Army, 29 July 2003.
15. Fiona Hill, 'Areas for Future Cooperation or Conflict in Central Asia and the Caucasus', Yale University Conference, 'The Silk Road in the 21st Century', 19 Sept. 2002.
16. Ibid.
17. Ibid.

Prospects For Russia-US Cooperation in Preventing WMD Proliferation

MIKHAIL POGORELY

Modern non-proliferation ideology and practice were born out of a broadly understood and loosely defined gut-feeling shared by the five original nuclear powers that existing weapons technologies are far too dangerous to be acquired by everyone wishing to acquire them. Thus, non-proliferation practice has been an attempt to keep outsiders as far away as possible from acquiring their own nuclear arsenals, and later other classes of weapons of mass destruction – chemical and biological.

Experts note that nuclear weapons raise the most telling issues: chemical and biological weapons are banned by international treaties, so the challenge they pose is basically one of enforcement. Nuclear weapons are temporarily legal in five countries, not illegal in three others and forbidden essentially everywhere else – a complex and inconsistent arrangement that presents a unique set of dilemmas and problems that are difficult to resolve, as a prominent US expert in this field, George Perkovich, describes the situation.[1]

The big issues here are who decides: who is responsible and deserves to have weapons of mass destruction (WMD), and who is not and should be restricted in this area. One side's good will may be seen as unfair and oppressive by another side and cause an unexpected or poorly understood reaction.

During the Cold War period, the 'Big Brothers', who also happened to be the major nuclear powers, had a calming effect on these differences. Their unique position in the world ensured that their word and will were perceived to have the force of law for the 'minors'. As Russia and the US increasingly find themselves on the same side of a barricade, they (and the world) encounter new dimensions and qualities in these old problems.

NON-PROLIFERATION TODAY

The pessimistic predictions of the early and mid-1990s that the struggle against proliferation and for strategic disarmament had been lost, and that these were agendas of the past, proved incorrect.

On the contrary, after a seven-year pause following the first G-8 summit (Moscow 1996), which focused on non-proliferation issues, world leaders again paid prime attention to these problems at the summits in Kananaskis (2002) and Evian (2003).

Despite widespread expectations that the George W. Bush administration would keep a low profile on arms control issues in the US-Russian agenda, the Cooperative Threat Reduction has moved forward in every aspect: WMD destruction assistance; physical protection of fissile materials and their account and control; plutonium production cut-off; and job security for scientists working in WMD-related areas.

In the spring of 2003 the world witnessed the first ever full-scale war where the basic motivation was proclaimed to be an attempt to stop illegal efforts to acquire WMD – chemical and biological weapons, and perhaps nuclear weapons, as well as missiles as delivery means.

After deep disappointment in the world, and particularly in Russia, due to the US's withdrawal from the 1972 ABM Treaty and the fact that START II was 'dead on arrival', the 2002 Moscow Strategic Offensive Reduction Treaty (SORT – a treaty on reductions in the strategic offensive arsenals of Russia and the US) became the first major arms-control treaty of the twenty-first century and demonstrated the good will of the two powers to cooperate as partners rather than competitors.

Yet the new era has also seen many horror tales from the past realized.

At least two states have 'blasted' their way into the ranks of the nuclear powers – India and Pakistan. In the latter case the world was as near as it had ever been to the first radical Islamic regime getting control of a nuclear arsenal. That situation arose when General Pervez Musharraf's government faced a powerful challenge from the radical opposition in the autumn of 2001, during the anti-Taliban military campaign in neighboring Afghanistan. The world was lucky that time.

A number of states have made public their wish to join either an official or de facto nuclear club in order to handle their defense tasks. But in most cases the purpose was to consolidate their political status in the world arena. The most dangerous development here is a chain reaction from the neighboring states.

International and national terrorist organizations have made WMD-terrorism a regular rather than an exotic practice – in the form of employing, or threatening to employ, chemical and biological agents, radiation or even nuclear devices, as well as attacking nuclear and chemical facilities. In most cases this has so far been a bluff. Yet the threat is very real, and the risk is not a hypothetical one.

The core problem of all non-proliferation issues is the difference in the angles from which the actors view the challenges and ways to meet them.

The US administration looks at the proliferation process as the transfer of technologies, parts, machines, fissile materials, chemical agents and so on, and their delivery means, from one state to one or more other states. The probability is very high that most export operations involving almost any sensitive technologies will make it onto a State Department or Defense Department list. The various agencies working to counteract such transfers will be viewed as non-proliferation agencies.

The same actions will be seen by the Russian administration as attempts to wage trade wars through dishonest means, pressuring an economic competitor by using state power, including political and military resources. For example, this is how Russian cooperation with India (missile engines) and Iran (the plant in Busher) has been treated.

The position of the Third World nations would differ from both of the aforementioned: they accent the political rather than the technological aspects of their potential nuclear status. First, this refers to the neo-imperialism of the resistant official nuclear nations and their self-proclaimed right to decide who deserves what. A half-century ago this situation may have been moral and just, or at least pragmatic. Yet in the modern global community there is a powerful trend to review the world order as established after World War II. Not only are several former 'developing countries' part of this movement (Brazil, India, Mexico, Nigeria, to name only a few), but so also are such influential nations as Germany and Japan.

Not that they want and are working to obtain their own WMD arsenals (with few exceptions). On the contrary, they all want a more secure world and insist that only strict adherence to existing arms-control and disarmament treaties will make such a secure world possible. Hence the heavy emphasis on Article VI of the 1968 Non-Proliferation Treaty (NPT), the provisions of which are often forgotten or ignored by the nuclear powers.

OLD MYTHOLOGY AND NEW THREATS

Realities of the new age, modern challenges prove that many efforts have been spent in vain because of false or at least wrong perceptions.

Despite all good (or otherwise) intentions, it has been impossible to maintain the closed nature of the nuclear club. At least three nations – the Republic of South Africa (RSA) in 1993, and India and Pakistan in 1998 – have declared that they have been able to design and produce nuclear weapons, and the RSA even to destroy them by 1991. Israel is believed to have achieved de facto nuclear status years ago and to have up to 200 warheads at its disposal.

All three of the still unofficial, or 'junior', members of the club develop their own national command-and-control structures and triads of delivery means, copying their 'elders'.

Belarus, Kazakhstan and Ukraine found themselves nuclear states overnight back in 1991 – even if unwillingly. In a case that was the subject of much speculation several years ago, that is, the success of General Lebed's separatist movement, his newly-founded Siberian Republic or Empire could have inherited the world's third largest nuclear arsenal (plus one of the world's two largest biological weapons labs).

On the other hand, only political restraints stand in the way of such nations as Argentina, Brazil, South Korea or Japan from developing and producing nuclear weapons.

For instance, an influential Japanese opposition leader, Ichiro Ozawa, has predicted Tokyo's possible and plausible reaction to any future aggressive stances taken by China (and perhaps North Korea, too). 'We have plenty of plutonium in our nuclear power plants, so it's possible for us to produce 3,000 to 4,000 nuclear warheads', he said.[2] These examples show that proliferation in the modern world results from political developments rather than from the technology transfers that are the focus of US attention.

Another myth that has long misled politicians and experts concerns the ability of large countries to control developments in WMD-related areas.

The events of September 11, 2001 in the US, worldwide Al-Qaeda activities, the WMD production/destruction situation in Iraq and the most recent developments in North Korea's nuclear military programs all vividly demonstrate the shortcomings of existing national intelligence methods, as well as the limited abilities of international organizations and bodies, including the International Atomic Energy Agency (IAEA) and numerous ad hoc committees.

Not only US agencies such as the CIA and DIA should be cited here. The Kelly case in Great Britain demonstrated that the British Secret Service's methods retain much of James Bond's heritage but often lack scientific depth of analysis. The Russian Federation's Foreign Intelligence Service also missed the birth and death of South Africa's bomb and failed to predict the Indian and Pakistani nuclear breakthrough.

Shortly before North Korea announced in April 2003 that it possessed a nuclear arsenal (which may range from two to five warheads or may also very well be a bluff – just a new aspect of notorious North Korean blackmail), Russian Atomic Energy Minister Alexander Rumyantsev stated that: 'It will take Pyongyang another 50 years to develop its own nuclear weapons'.[3]

Even more problematic is control over export and import operations involving sensitive technologies and expertise. The most recent survey of US defense-related exports, performed by the Department of State, shows a 12 per cent rate (50 out of 428 cases examined) of illegal use of weapons and technologies by consumers that are US trade partners, of which 34 per cent were West European nations and 26 per cent Middle Eastern. East Asian Pacific and Latin American countries accounted for 20 per cent each. Illegal use includes, for example, unauthorized transfer of defense articles to third parties that might be involved in unfriendly activities against the US or its partners.[4]

This is most probably also true in the case of the Russian Federation and other nuclear powers and countries with missile technologies. Now all the more so, since there is a trend to move nuclear technologies to the private sector in Russia. Currently this concerns only the atomic energy sector, and mostly the production of reactors themselves and some equipment.

But certainly the new situation in Russia causes a problem, still a hypothetical one, wherein a production facility itself sets the technological standards for its products and there are no legal barriers against design 'variations' that will enable exploiters to produce sufficient weapons-grade plutonium. Another aspect of this problem is that privately-owned Russian facilities today run nuclear power station projects for China and India, and they might also take over the contract with Iran.[5]

There are those in Russia who say that privatization of the nuclear energy sector is only healthy for the national economy and has no dangerous aspects, as long as the state controls the nuclear fuel cycle. Without nuclear fuel, of course, reactors are dead, and uranium fuel is under strict state control (by the Atomic Energy Ministry – Minatom). Or should be, at least.

In fact, despite all the measures that have been taken, more than 250 incidents occurred at nuclear fuel facilities in the Soviet Union and Russia between 1949 and 2000, of which the new Russian Federation's share from 1993 to 2000 was 39 incidents. No fewer than 14 incidents occurred between 1996 and 2001 during the transport of fresh or spent fuel by highway, railway or river.[6]

Another point: the private economy always finds ways to circumvent strict state controls and trade barriers. For instance, it was reported that during closed Senate hearings in September 2002, evidence was revealed on 24 US companies, such as Hewlett Packard, Textronics, TI Coating, International Computer Systems, and others, exporting numerous defense-related equipment to Iraq from 1985 to 1988. During the same period hazardous biological materials such as anthrax and botulinum toxin were transferred to Iraqi experts by US bio-labs in Atlanta, Georgia, and Manass, Virginia. And up to 11 US companies, including Honeywell, Rockwell, Bechtel and Sperry, according to data from European experts, took part in enhancing Iraq's nuclear military program.

Thus, very often state agencies look in the wrong directions in search of the sources and channels of proliferation and ways to close them.

Another mistake, or at least a very serious reason for the malfunctioning of mechanisms designed to prevent and deny WMD proliferation, is an incorrect emphasis on various classes of WMD. As a result, nuclear weapons get much more attention than they deserve – while biological and especially chemical agents, receive much less attention they than should.

This has led to a situation in which most WMD-related political and military actions are aimed at controlling (in one way or another) nuclear weapons only, when the public and the media are concerned mostly with existing nuclear arsenals, and when various official bodies and non-governmental organizations combat primarily nuclear proliferation and try to prevent it.

This shift of attention is presumably rooted in the psychological effect of nuclear weapons, based on their visible and devastating power. Yet in reality biological and chemical weapons may be just as dangerous, especially when used against civilians in heavily populated areas. In this case the psychological impact even surpasses the combat effects of these weapons. Tiny quantities of anthrax, many times less then used in a single warhead, almost paralyzed the US in the autumn of 2001 and caused serious psychological trauma to thousands of Americans.

And of course chemical agents are much easier to produce or acquire than nuclear devices and weapons. It is believed that 16 countries today have access to chemical weapons know-how.

The attractiveness these weapons hold for states and terrorists far exceeds the attention they receive both in the disarmament process and in attempts to prevent proliferation of the technologies and production base.

DIRECTIONS OF PROLIFERATION

Proliferation is normally understood as 'new cells added.' In the case of WMD that means the spread of such weapons and/or the technologies for their production, delivery and combat use. Correspondingly, there are three major dimensions of WMD proliferation: horizontal, vertical, internal.

Horizontal proliferation, that is, adding new states that own nuclear, chemical and biological weapons and delivery means, such as missiles, submarines, aircraft, and so on, receives the highest attention by the US administration. Year after year this threat tops the list of threats to US national security presented by the Central Intelligence Director.

Russia and China are traditionally among the proliferators, while North Korea, Iran, Libya and Iraq are named as countries seeking to gain WMD access. One hopes that in the next report Iraq will only have mention as a historical precedent.

In practice there has been no sound evidence of any of these nations doing anything illegal, yet plenty of official Washington's suspicions about the bad intentions of proliferators have been made public. Some of those vociferous media campaigns end in great confusion, such as the situation in Iraq where no evidence has been found that the state was really involved in secret and illegal WMD research and production, which had been the core of every pre-war report on Iraq and US-Iraqi relations.

The aim in most cases has been to impress the general public and to influence public opinion, even though serious experts understand that each time 'reporters were dancing to the tune their government sources played (shunning in the process, the pursuit of any facts that might annoy the authorities)'.[7] The news media and numerous NGOs have scored high marks in this patriotism test.

Official Russian reaction to real or imaginary (though plausible) proliferation cases has been traditionally low profile. Even when India and Pakistan openly declared their nuclear status, Russian leaders were very unspecific, speaking in general terms about the need to take responsible steps toward strengthening nuclear security in the world. This position was echoed by the media and non-governmental experts.

The reason behind a lack of interest in this aspect of proliferation is rooted in the fact that Russia has viewed only the US as a major potential adversary. Unlike the Americans or the Japanese, very few people in Russia care about North Korean nukes and missiles, or about Iranian nukes – again, unlike the Americans and the Israelis.

Today Russia has no official adversaries, including the US and other NATO countries. However, these countries are not among Russia's official friends, either. So, concerns about these countries' security are typically formal and come up during Russian-US, Russian-British, or Russian-Italian etc., summits, but they have not, at least so far, been given substance in the *National Security Concept, Military Doctrine, Information Security Doctrines* or similar official documents.

Sometimes President Putin advises not paying too much attention to those documents, yet none of them has been revoked or revised since he assumed Russia's highest position of authority.

Vertical proliferation causes qualitatively different reactions in Moscow, Washington, and elsewhere. Vertical proliferation normally refers to the process of modifying and improving existing WMD, adding new designs and models to a nation's arsenal and increasing quantities in a given country.

Russian experts view this type of proliferation as very significant for the fate of arms control and disarmament, probably more so
than horizontal proliferation. They opine that better designs of
weapons systems (whether offensive or defensive) break the existing balance of potentials and thus provoke responsive actions among
counterparts. Some 95 per cent of the publications and public
speeches by Russian political and military leaders on the subject of
the US national missile defense plans contain a paragraph stating that
the newest Russian Topol-M missile is still capable of penetrating
future US defenses.

Most US politicians and many experts with ties to the current
administration do not view vertical proliferation as harmful to
national and international politics. They champion such major
WMD-related initiatives of the George W. Bush administration as:

- Readiness to resort to nuclear weapons in response to an
  enemy's use of, or intention to use, chemical or biological
  weapons, formulated in last year's *National Security Presidential
  Directive (NSPD 17)*;
- Readiness to use nuclear weapons in conventional conflicts
  involving Iran, Syria, Libya, Iraq, and in support of US allies in
  possible conflicts on the Korean peninsula or between China and
  Taiwan, as expressed in the latest *Nuclear Posture Review* of
  2002;
- An attempt to repeal the 1993 congressional prohibition against
  developing, testing and producing new small nuclear weapons
  (bunker busters and, probably, NMD-related anti-missile warheads);
- Lack of willingness to support ratification of the Comprehensive
  Test Ban Treaty and, on the contrary, readiness to resume underground nuclear tests (to examine the reliability and physical
  characteristics of stored weapons and create new-generation
  ones).[8]

The following is a statement on new-weapons research and
production plans typical for the current administration and its
military and science experts. Says Paul Robinson, director of Sandia
National Laboratories and a former chief negotiator at the US-USSR
nuclear testing talks in Geneva: 'That depends on how you define
"new". If we take a warhead off the shelf that we designed and
tested in the past, and then put it on a new delivery vehicle, is that
a new weapon? We will probably have to manufacture new copies

because we produced only a few originally, but it is not a new design, nor will we need to test it'.[9]

Just imagine the US reaction to a hypothetical situation in which, say, India would take its current 800-mile missiles' warheads and place them on a 'new delivery vehicle' with an 8,000-mile range. Or Russia producing extra mini-nukes ('suitcase bombs') that are not prohibited by existing treaties. For sure, there would be many questions as to why these nations need new (no quotation marks!) weapons and against whom they plan to use them.

Another point, the matter of the first or, even more so the preemptive, use of nuclear weapons is a worry to those who are concerned about the future of the non-proliferation movement, including the US's closest allies. Hiroshima Mayor Tadatoshi Akiba says the Non-Proliferation Treaty is 'on the verge of collapse', not because of North Korean actions, but because the US is 'openly declaring the possibility of a preemptive nuclear first strike'.[10]

While this is not an official US nuclear policy, the above-mentioned *NSPD-17* endorses a strategy of preemption against the WMD of a potential enemy, and the Pentagon's *Nuclear Posture Review* lays out contingencies under which so-called 'useable nuclear weapons' may be employed. 'Usable' in this context means theater/tactical nuclear weapons (they are believed to have been considered for use during both Persian Gulf campaigns of 1990–91 and 2003).

The level of acceptance is very clearly described by Robinson, of Sandia National Laboratories. He says that, 'A national command authority confronted in a crisis with the prospect of killing 40,000 people with a thermo-nuclear weapon in order to take out a bunker is probably going to decide not to. If we could design a bunker-buster that would kill an estimated 2,000 to 3,000 people, on the other hand, the answer would probably be yes if the situation was critical'.[11]

Seeing how much the nuclear states care about their 'big sticks' ('If Russia has no nuclear arsenal – there's no nation, no power', opines Lev Ryabev, one of the best known Russian nuclear weapons experts of the two latest decades), other nations strive to raise their political status and defense capabilities by adding WMD to their inventories.[12] Regardless of the price. Former Pakistani President Zia ul-Haq was reported to say, 'We shall eat grass but will build the bomb'. Which they did. His current Indian counterpart A.P.J. Abdul Kalam echoes this idea: 'Nations consist of people, and with their effort, a nation can accomplish all it could ever want'.[13]

Since this is considered true, we should also acknowledge the harsh reality of WMD terrorism's coming of age. Even though terrorist organizations are not 'nations', today they represent large transnational organizations, financed and equipped often beyond the level of many national armies.

Internal proliferation is the term offered by the author to describe the possibility of nuclear, chemical and biological weapons, materials and technologies getting into the hands of terrorist organizations or individuals.

Russian authorities have traditionally ruled out such a scenario, while US authorities and experts have viewed it as a plausible (almost inevitable) reality. This is the most probable major driving force behind the Cooperative Threat Reduction program pursued by the US to provide assistance to former Soviet republics in securing their hazardous materials and technologies.

On the contrary, Russian experts maintain that the old nuclear powers have built safe and reliable command-and-control systems overseeing their WMD arsenals – unlike the new, semi-official nuclear powers. The latter's nuclear weapons stand the highest risk of being seized or destroyed by terrorists.

Experts also consider nuclear power stations to be rich targets for terrorists. There is much room for perfection in the current state of security at such facilities both in the US and in Russia. The press has carried many reports on this problem in the US, including on measures to test and to raise the security of nuclear energy facilities.

Russian authorities usually assure the nation and the world that Russian nuclear power stations are sufficiently protected to withstand attack a dozen terrorists. Experts go further and acknowledge that a company-size formation (80–100 people) could take control of a civilian nuclear objective and either destroy it or use it to blackmail local or federal authorities.

The only nuclear power station built in Russia (as opposed to Soviet-built facilities) is the one at Volgodonsk, which was the first to be commissioned after the 30 December 1999 Presidential Order N1772, *On the State system of preventing and combating nuclear terrorism and its consequences*, took effect.[14] Because of its proximity to the North Caucasian 'theater of war', the public views every aspect of that station's security with more scrutiny than anywhere in Russia.

Minatom was proud to report that new security systems interdict pedestrian and motorized terrorists infiltrating the station perimeter.

And the then first Deputy Minister Valentin Ivanov informed the public that the reactor was protected against any airplane crashing down onto it. However, the station's security service chief added additional details: the reactor would resist the impact only of an object weighing up to 20 tons and flying no faster than 800 km/h. (500 mph).[15] Almost any fighter plane is both heavier and faster, to say nothing of passenger and cargo jets.

Chemical weapons present an even greater threat, as both targets and loot for terrorists. They are poorly guarded at storage and destruction facilities. On the other hand, they can be a thousand times easier to produce than nukes. Last autumn a mere chemistry academy student in Moscow managed to design a home-made bomb and to plant it in the heart of Moscow, just a quarter mile away from the Kremlin. He claimed to be connected to radical neo-bolsheviks, which he hardly was. Yet any other academic could take his place.

There are thousands of other scientists with the expertise to design and produce a WMD device, primitive perhaps, but workable. For example, for years the people of Sarov supported a Communist candidate in the Duma elections, which means there are plenty of people unhappy with the current regime and theoretically able to lend a helping hand to the regime's opponents.

TRADITIONAL AND NEW TOOLS

This brings us to methods for practical implementation of a non-proliferation regime and ideas. There's a mix of traditional and new tools here. How do they work and are all of them effective?

Best known and most popular of the traditional tools is the Non-Proliferation Treaty (NPT) of 1968, extended in 1995 and reviewed in 2002. It next comes up for review in 2005. The big nuclear powers speak much of the NPT's significance, yet they tend to ignore the spirit of the treaty. That causes a certain uneasiness on the part of other nations who look jealously at every move of Washington and Moscow in WMD-related areas and pay particular attention to their compliance with the letter and spirit of Article VI of the NPT.

Take the 2002 Moscow Treaty. Although both the White House and the Kremlin cite it as a major contribution to implementing the Article VI provisions (it states, in particular, that 'Each of the Parties to the Treaty undertakes to pursue negotiations in good faith on effective measures relating to cessation of the nuclear arms race at an early date and to nuclear disarmament'.), this agreement has plenty of critics. They suggest that the treaty is aimed more at beefing up the peacemaking image of the signatories than at really making the world more secure.

The critics quote provisions of the 2002 SORT which require that the nuclear arsenal of the US and Russia be cut to 1,700–2,200 'operationally deployed' warheads by 31 December 2012 – yet the class of weapons is not defined, nor is a timetable for such a scale-down provided. This means that the current 5,500–6,000-warhead levels will remain legal until the aforementioned date, and the next day the treaty expires and becomes history. There is also an extremely simple procedure for withdrawing from the treaty, which requires only that a letter of notification be provided three months prior to walking out – any day any party wants that.[16]

Along with their lack of will to comply seriously with the provisions of Article VI, the selectiveness of the nuclear powers, namely the US and Russia, makes other nations skeptical about the future of non-proliferation process. This selectiveness is seen when the two powers consider equally important the whole set of existing nuclear security treaties and ongoing negotiations and attempts to reach agreement on such issues as the Comprehensive Test Ban Treaty, the Fissile Material Cutoff Treaty, the Non-Strategic Nuclear Weapons Ban Treaty, and so on.

Here's just one example of arguments used to substantiate such selectiveness. Says US Secretary of Energy Abraham Spencer: 'We must...give our weapons scientists the resources and authority to explore advanced weapons concepts, including research related to low-yield weapons. Funding constraints and confusing legal prohibitions have stifled most new thinking on these issues. This has, in turn, made us less capable of devising the best responses to emerging threats'.[17] Absolutely symmetrical ideas are appreciated by Russian nuclear scientists (politicians tend to keep silent on issues of presidential responsibilities).

Bilateral measures (other than disarmament agreements) also belong to the old set of non-proliferation tools. They are easier to change and adjust to new administrations' demands and political priorities. The Cooperative Threat Reduction (CTR) framework agreements provide the best example.

According to State Department official Sherwood McGinnis, deputy US representative to the Conference on Disarmament, the

US has, for more than a decade, engaged in a huge program of cooperation with the states of the former Soviet Union to address the 'threat posed by the Cold War legacy of WMD programs'. That program, which has to date been allocated a total of $8 billion – with another $1 billion requested for fiscal year 2004 – has helped to eliminate about 900 ballistic missiles, more than 100 bombers and almost 50 ballistic submarines. Furthermore, it has redirected into civilian programs the skills and efforts of thousands of scientists formerly involved in WMD activities.[18]

More precise figures of CTR accomplishments as of May 2003 are offered by the Russian-American Nuclear Security Advisory Council:[19]

Nuclear warheads deactivated	6,032
ICBMs destroyed	506
ICBM silos eliminated	438
ICBM mobile launchers destroyed	1
Ballistic missile submarines destroyed	26
SLBMs eliminated	382
SLBM launchers eliminated	408
Strategic bombers eliminated	109
Nuclear air-to-surface missiles destroyed	554
Nuclear test holes/tunnels sealed	194

This is on the positive side of the CTR programs. On the negative side, some experts feel that the US is seeking to disarm Russia. They cite, for example, the latest US moves to close the Russian plutonium producing reactors at Seversk and Zheleznogorsk. The US administration announced in May 2003 that it is providing Russia with $466 million of support to comply with this task. Yet it is known that the US administration has announced that it will have to resume production of plutonium needed to refresh triggers of nuclear warheads in the US inventory. The cost of the project is expected to run from $2.2 billion to $4.4 billion, and actual production is expected to start no sooner than 2020.[20] Some Russian experts fear that in accepting certain US assistance today, Russia will have to pay a much higher price to deal with the national problems of tomorrow.

Almost the same arguments are heard from those who oppose the US-supported option of doing away with existing Russian stockpiles of weapon-grade plutonium – that is, burying it after turning it into a glass mass at the Mayak facility in Ozersk. Opponents prefer burning it in the form of MOX fuel in breeder (fast neutron) reactors, and note that plutonium is extremely valuable fissile material that might be kept intact for future generations.

One of the problems with the CTR and other bilateral US-Russian programs, inter-governmental and non-governmental, is an inadequate presentation of their goals and intentions, as well as Russia's interests in them, to the Russian public (though this may be true for the US side as well, according to evidence from the author's colleagues in the US). CTR-related programs and major Nuclear Treaty Initiatives lack press coverage – the author on a number of occasions has challenged Senators Sam Nunn and Richard Lugar to pay special attention to this issue, with little effect.

Another problem concerning the effectiveness of CTR programs is the lack of a single 'CTR program' – the assistance efforts of various donor-agencies (the US Department of State, Department of Defense and Department of Energy, with some assistance from the side of FBI, CIA, NRC and other agencies) are widely dispersed across as many as 40 recipients in Russia. Sometimes they are referred to by a common name, the 'Nunn-Lugar program', but in reality there are a variety of unrelated programs, such as nuclear and chemical weapons destruction assistance; making fissile materials storage secure, and transporting and eliminating them; the nuclear cities initiative; jobs offers for scientists working in weapons-related fields, and so on.

Of course, a single federal program is in no way a panacea, but it helps at least to draw a unified inter-agency picture of the US assistance in the Russian disarmament process (though perhaps the government fears such a comprehensive picture).

Some new counter-proliferation tools should be mentioned. Unlike more or less passive attempts to prevent non-authorized nations from obtaining nuclear weapons and technologies, counter-proliferation is supposed to employ very active enforcement methods, going as far as waging war against any proliferating nation.

Previously such practice was scarcely legal: the Israeli destruction of an Iraqi nuclear reactor was not supported by the major world powers. Today waging a war against a proliferating nation is a fairly normal practice, and politicians discuss whether the Bush administration will launch combat actions against Iran before or after the 2004 presidential elections – but not the option of a military action against Iran per se.

Today this practice finds more support from Russia when it is tied to the problem of combating international terrorism. The trade-off is obviously the Chechen problem set as an integral part of worldwide anti-terrorist activities in the global community.

Another condition suggests that Russia is an equal partner in the decision-making process. For instance, the *Foreign Policy Concept of the Russian Federation* sets the goal of Russia's strategy on the Korean peninsula, 'to focus efforts on ensuring Russia's equal participation in solving the Korean problem', rather than seeking a certain specific result.[21]

Another new tool for solving non-proliferation problems is bringing these issues to top-level summits. Traditionally, nuclear security and safety were discussed at US-Soviet and US-Russian bilateral summits. The first ever multilateral non-proliferation summit took place in Moscow in April 1996, but its main aim was to outline the modern dimensions of the problem and adopt a declaration citing mutual goals.

Only last year in Kananaskis, and this year in Evian, leaders of the G-8 nations set specific goals, timetables and financial milestones to help Russia do away with its Cold War-era WMD legacy. This task is simultaneously a major contribution to the global non-proliferation process, because due to mounting technical, technological, financial and social problems, Russia continues to remain the most dangerous place on the planet – and from the point of view of WMD proliferation as well.

The US has pledged to invest $10 billion in this program, compared with Russia's own $2 billion, with an additional $1.7 billion from Germany, $1.2 billion from Italy, $883 million from France, $750 million from the UK, $727 million from Canada, $200 million from Japan, $14 million from Norway, $13 million from Switzerland, $0.5 million from Sweden and $1.2 billion from the European Union.[22]

POSSIBILITIES AND CHANCES FOR THE FUTURE

So, what are the possibilities for further US-Russian cooperation in WMD non-proliferation, and what are the chances that they will be realized?

There remains much room to continue cooperation on a multi-lateral basis, but this requires greater US attention to treaties that are vital to the international non-proliferation movement, such as the

Comprehensive Test Ban Treaty (CTBT), the Fissile Material Cut-off Treaty (FMCT) and the like. The 2005 NPT review conference will provide a good opportunity to review US national policy concerning nuclear tests as well – given that the US is not really going to produce a new generation of nuclear weapons, including space-based weapons. North Korea's withdrawal from the NPT sets a dangerous precedent, and the NPT should be supported by emphasis on the CTBT.

Unfortunately, this does not look realistic until at least 2010–12. During this period Britain, France and China are not likely to join the nuclear arms reduction process. It is even less likely that India, Pakistan and China will do so. There are chances, however, that new de facto nuclear powers will emerge in the first decade of the twenty-first century, such as Iran, Taiwan, one or both Korean states, and perhaps even Germany and Japan.

None of the new nuclear nations will be able to challenge the world leadership in the first decade of the century, yet each of them may be a regional leader and might need WMD as a status tool, if not as weapons per se.

The US and Russia have a good chance to continue bilateral cooperation both in downsizing WMD threats originating from Russia and in combating the proliferation process in third nations that are subject to the traditional influence of Russia and the US. Iran and North Korea are the best examples for Russia, as are Taiwan or South Korea for the US.

The CTR programs' future is destined to be a success story. Russia is vitally interested in continued US assistance, otherwise she would not be able to cope with the burden of WMD elimination. Only the Russian Navy still has 193 decommissioned nuclear submarines afloat, 89 of them with irradiated nuclear fuel in their reactors. Minatom sees absolutely no way to solve this problem without foreign assistance.[23]

Interestingly, despite all the help from the US side, the military establishment and the general public still tend to view the US as rather an aggressive state and the most plausible adversary of Russia. A leading public opinion polling agency, VTsIOM, reported on the eve of the Iraq war that in March 2003 no less than 71 per cent of respondents considered the US a prime threat to peace and security on Earth, while only 45 per cent cited Iraq as posing such a threat, and North Korea 21 per cent, as compared with six per cent of

Russians thinking that Russia herself poses a major threat to peace in the world.[24]

This once again shows the importance of providing the nation and society with balanced, unbiased information. The state-owned or controlled media are not up to this task. The NGO community that covers issues of nuclear security and WMD proliferation, including international cooperation in this sphere, is limited in numbers (no more than a dozen Russian NGOs and half a dozen foreign NGO offices with Russian activities) and has not yet gained enough experience or, therefore, influence.[25]

US and Russian NGO cooperation is one of the best channels for contributing to the non-proliferation process through exchange of expertise and ideas that might help to shape Russian national policy.

Coming back to the issue of the Russian public's misperception of the US policy, it is important to understand that the roots of this phenomenon are not necessarily in this policy's 'aggressiveness'. More often they lie in the indecisiveness of Russia's own political strategy. Even top Moscow diplomats and other decision-makers do not often know what they want or how they are going to react to newly emerging challenges of the modern world.

It is difficult to believe, but the entire paragraph covering Russian-Iranian relations in the second most significant document defining Russian international strategy (after the Constitution), the *Foreign Policy Concept*, runs as follows: 'It is important to continue developing relations with Iran'.[26]

Yet it is more or less certain that Russia will not join future Iraq-like counter-proliferation enforcement actions, unless Moscow sees a clear and present danger for Russia stemming from proliferating nations and has sound evidence of illegal activities.

Still, the absence or small scale of other common interests (especially economic ones – trade, joint manufacturing, investments, etc.), other than joint space-research projects, will force US and Russian leaders to keep proliferation and counter-proliferation issues on the agenda of their summits until at least the end of the decade.

Several years ago Moscow's political and military leaders insisted on nuclear-security contacts with Washington because this seemed to be the most developed and reliable channel for communication between the two nations. Today this seems to be one of the few remaining channels at all.

But the channel of communication based on military confrontation and, subsequently, cooperation, perhaps should be replaced with anti-crime, anti-terrorist and security-police agenda channels that may be more in US and Russian interests in the years to come.

NOTES

1. George Perkovich, 'Bush's Nuclear Revolution: A Regime Change in Nonproliferation', Carnegie Endowment for International Peace *Proliferation Brief*, Vol. 6, No. 4, 13 March 2003.
2. Howard W. French, 'Nuclear Arms Taboo is Challenged in Japan', *The New York Times*, 9 June 2002.
3. Armen Hanbabyan, 'Modest Affection of an A-Bomb' (in Russian), *Novaya Model*, 5 Dec. 2002.
4. 'FY 2002 End-Use Monitoring of Defense Articles and Defense Services Commercial Exports', <www.pmdtc.org/docs/End_Use_FY2002.pdf>.
5. Vladimir Gubarev, 'Nuclear Heart Secrets. An Interview with Yury Dragunov, the 'Hydropress' Special Design Bureau Director-Designer General' (in Russian), *Literaturnaya Gazeta*, 14–20 May 2003.
6. See Vladimir Kuznetsov, *Major Problems and Current State of Security at Nuclear Fuel Cycle Facilities of the Russian Federation* (in Russian), (Moscow: The Green Cross of Russia; The Center for War and Peace Journalism 2002).
7. Linda Rothstein, 'Loyal to a Fault', *Bulletin of the Atomic Scientists*, Vol. 59, No. 4 (July/Aug. 2003).
8. John Isaacs, 'Congress Jumps Off the Ban Wagon', *Bulletin of the Atomic Scientists*, Vol. 59, No. 4 (July/Aug. 2003).
9. James Kitfield, 'The Pros and Cons of New Nuclear Weapons', *National Journal*, 9 Aug. 2003.
10. Ralph A. Cossa, 'Rethinking US Nuclear Strategy', *Global Beat Syndicate*, 25 Aug. 2003.
11. Kitfield (note 9).
12. Vladimir Gubarev, 'Nuclear Apostle' (in Russian), *Literaturnaya Gazeta*, 3–9 Sept. 2003.
13. David Rohde, 'Nuclear Scientist, 70, a Folk Hero is Elected India's President', *The New York Times*, 19 July 2002.
14. A.M. Agapov, G.A. Novikov and A.P. Panfilov, 'The State of Security and Readiness to Meet Extraordinary Situations at Facilities of Minatom of Russia' (in Russian), *Nuclear and Radiation Security of Russia*, Issue 2(9), 2003.
15. Tatiana Ivanova, 'Thy Sky Over NPS is Safe' (in Russian), *The Global Security Issues*, No. 11 (May/June 2003).
16. See Articles I and IV of the *Strategic Offensive Reductions Treaty*, <www.whitehouse gov/news/releases/2002/05/20020524–3.html>.
17. Abraham Spencer, 'Facing a New Nuclear Reality', *The Washington Post*, 21 July 2003.
18. <usinfo.state.gov/topical/pol/arms/03050503.htm>.

19. Michael Roston and David Smigielski, 'Accomplishments of Selected Threat Reduction and Non-Proliferation Programs in Russia, By Agency', *Nuclear New*, 10 June 2003, <www.ransac.org/Documents/060103_accomplishments.pdf>.
20. Associated Press, 'U.S. Will Resume Production of Nuclear Warhead Triggers', *The New York Times*, 2 June 2002.
21. <www.ln.mid.ru/B1.nsf/arh/1EC8DC08180306614325699C003B5FF0?Open Document>.
22. *A Post-Evian Assessment*. Issue No. 1, July 2003, CSIS. <www.sgpproject.org/gpupdate/1.htm>.
23. Proceedings of the 'Ecological and Informational Security' international conference, Moscow, 8–12 Sept. 2003.
24. 'The Symmetric War' (in Russian), *Literaturnaya Gazeta*, 2–8 April 2003.
25. See Roland Timerbayev and Anton Khlopkov, 'Scientific Research Centers and Non-Governmental Organizations Covering Issues of WMD Non-Proliferation, Arms Control and Disarmament' (in Russian), *Scientific Notes by PIR-Center*, No. 2 (23), 2003.
26. <www.ln.mid.ru/B1.nsf/arh/1EC8DC08180306614325699C003B5FF0?Open Document>.

Prospects for US-Russian Cooperation in Ballistic Missile Defense and Outer Space Activities

ALEXANDER G. SAVELYEV

Space presents realistic opportunities for US-Russian cooperation. But how can the two countries cooperate while also protecting their own national interests? Can the US afford to go it alone in space? What will be the long-term effect of the commercialization of space? Faced with ever declining space-technology budgets, Russia needs international cooperation if its space industry is to survive. At the same time, the US has shifted its interests away from cooperation and toward the military aspects of space. Further, the author says, the US has been inclined to solve problems unilaterally. But the author contends that the US is critically dependent on Russian launchers and that both countries would benefit from mutual efforts and expertise. Potential areas for joint work include ballistic-missile defense, protecting space-based systems, and data exchange on space objects. All of the foregoing, the author notes, would support national and international security.

The history of cooperation in outer space between the US and the USSR, and the US and Russia, proves that successful and effective joint work between the two leading space states is possible and that it can lead to implementation of different space-related projects of various levels.

But despite the fact that since the early 1990s the geo-political situation has opened qualitatively new perspectives for cooperation among the participants in space exploration, there are still more questions than answers regarding partnership between the US and Russia. These questions include: how to achieve a high level of effectiveness in this cooperation while preserving each partner's national interests? How can this cooperation contribute to global stability? What role can the partnership play in developing space-based information and communication systems for the creation of a new framework of strategic stability? How will the process of the 'commercialization' of space activities affect the development of the US-Russian strategic partnership, including the creation of space-based information systems with the characteristics comparable to those of military devices?

Yet, most of these questions do not have a unanimous answer. Moreover, there exist quite opposite points of view on the prospects for US-Russian cooperation in this area. The reason is the growing gap in the two states' technical and economic capabilities, as well as the still lingering uncertainties about the very nature of the strategic relations between our countries. Quite naturally, none of these factors help stimulate partnership relations between Russia and the US in either commercial or military fields of space exploration. Nevertheless, in my view, the potential for such cooperation remains high. If the parties can overcome existing difficulties and differences, this potential can be implemented with a relatively high level of effectiveness.

RUSSIAN POTENTIAL

The Russian space industry, unlike many others, possesses very favorable opportunities and potential for entering the world market. Starting in about 1993, Russia's participation in international space programs and projects became a very important factor for the development of Russian space programs and also a necessary condition for it. It was international cooperation that helped preserve the space branch of Russian industry in a situation where state support of space activities was constantly declining. Thus, between 1989 and 2002, state support for space activities declined by 20 times. At the same time, this industry's share in the GDP fell from 0.73 per cent in 1989 to 0.12 per cent in 2001.[1] Thus, at present international cooperation in outer space is one of the main directions of the activities of the Russian Aerospace Agency ('Rosaviakosmos'). This cooperation covers practically all the activities mentioned in the Federal Space Program of Russia.[2]

In spite of these serious financial difficulties, for the foreseeable future (until at least the end of the next decade) Russia still has a good chance of preserving its place among the leading space states of the world.

The Russian missile and space industry has always been a place of concentration of the most modern technologies. In the early 1990s the former USSR occupied a leading position in approximately 50 per cent of space technologies. During the 1990s period of economic crisis, Russia lost many of these technologies (around 300 technologies, according to some estimates), as well as time and rates of development. But the potential of the space technology branch remains high. Thus, Russian achievements in engines that use different fuel types, electrical systems, orbital stations, composition materials, hydrogen technologies and others, are well known. In addition, there are still heavy 'intellectual investments' in the sphere of advanced technologies, including adaptive optics, and others. Today many experts predict a coming multifaceted technological breakthrough in space technologies. If Russia devotes more attention to space technologies, it will be able to maintain its leading role in some of them.

At present (2002) Rosaviakosmos' annual program is approximately 35 times lower than NASA's budget, and 3.5 times lower than the annual budget of the European Space Agency as approved for the period 2002–06. In the US, the annual space budget is about 80 billion dollars; in Japan – 3.6 billion dollars; in Europe – 3 billion dollars; in France – 2.5 billion dollars; China – 1.9 billion dollars; and in India – 0.55 billion dollars; but in Russia – only 0.193 billion dollars[3]. So, the characteristic feature of the present stage of Russian space activities is that financial support is not consistent with the real potential of this branch.

We can offer some figures to prove this conclusion. If we take the total of the US and Russian figures and represent space activities as 100 per cent, we see the following picture for 2000:[4]

Non-military space budget: Russia – 9%; US – 91%;
Number of satellites in orbit: Russia – 22%; US – 78%;
Overall spending on space activities up to 1997: Russia – 38%; US – 62%;
Overall spending on land-based infrastructure up to 1997: Russia – 43%; US – 57%;
Satellite launch capabilities (annual): Russia – 67%; US – 33%.

US-RUSSIAN PARTNERSHIP IN OUTER SPACE

After quite an optimistic stage of space cooperation between 1993 and 2000, when such projects as the international orbit station, the sea-launch system and others took place, the current situation in US-Russian non-military cooperation in outer space could be described, if not as stagnation, as uncertainty. One can say that the optimism of the 1990s was not realized. Moreover, beginning with the new millennium the US obviously lost interest in cooperation in space with Russia, having shifted its attention to the military aspects of space exploration. It is symbolic that, for the first time, in May 2002, issues of US-Russian cooperation in outer space received practically no reflection in the final documents of the summit of the two presidents (G. Bush and V. Putin).

After the 'Discovery' tragedy, the US began to pay more attention to the prospects for US-Russian cooperation in this sphere. Thus, according to the US Deputy Secretary of State for Arms Control, S. Redmaker, the US is critically dependent on Russian launchers.[5] Nevertheless the real prospects for such cooperation remain unclear.

A number of factors play a negative role in this situation. The Russian-American Commission on Economic and Technical Cooperation, established in April 1993 (at a summit in Vancouver), has ceased to exist. Issues of the US-Russian partnership in outer space occupied a very serious place in the agenda of this commission.[6] Throughout the 1990s this commission played the role of the main coordinating body for US-Russian cooperation in outer space.

Another negative factor is the passivity of the Special Committee on Prevention of An Arms Race in Outer Space – PAROS.[7] This committee was established back in 1985 within the framework of the Conference on Disarmament. The activity of this committee is all but blocked, since the participants still cannot reach a consensus on the format of the negotiations.

Finally, the most important factor preventing further development of the US-Russian cooperation in this sphere is the position of the US. The US still does not express much interest in this issue and attempts to solve the main problems unilaterally.[8]

It is absolutely clear that the US has great superiority in space technology and possesses the most modern scientific, technical and industrial base in this area. Nevertheless, one should not consider this superiority a constant factor. Technical changes under circumstances of rapid scientific progress, accompanied by political and military factors, as well as the increasing importance of space systems for all aspects of the development of other countries (many of which try to obtain independent capabilities for space exploration), can lead to a situation in which the US not only changes its position on these issues, but also loses its number-one place in this area.

One should mention that the list of potential areas of US-Russian cooperation in outer space can be quite long. Thus, in the sphere of information alone there are potential projects in the following areas, among others: developing a global space information security system; joint efforts to reduce the vulnerability of space-based systems; joint analysis and data exchange on space objects; the protection of 'space information streams'; joint monitoring of informational threats to space systems; and monitoring the space in general (including radiation, intensity of the 'sun wind', the characteristics of the magnetic field and other factors which influence the transmission of information to and from space), and so on.

The realization of prospective space technologies will make it possible to begin implementing large civil space projects by the end of the next decade. For example, a large portion of the efforts will go toward developing 'great space energy' programs, whose goal is to prevent a coming energy and environmental crisis. In this connection, building and using orbital solar power stations and transmitting energy to the earth will be on the agenda of international cooperation in outer space. Space technologies can also help solve the problem of 'weather control', including the control of typhoons, and other unpleasant 'surprises'. According to the views of some Russian experts, lasers under development for military use could also be used for such purposes. In particular, the Russian Rocket and Space Corporation, 'Energia' (Energy), is studying such possibilities.[9]

In addition to the aforementioned, a number of other projects, such as 'space isolation' of nuclear and toxic waste, counter-meteorite programs, production in space and others have good prospects. After 2020 manned flights to Mars and the construction of moon bases will also sound much less fantastic than today.

RUSSIA'S COOPERATION IN OUTER SPACE WITH OTHER COUNTRIES

During the past ten years the scale of Russia's international cooperation in outer space activities has grown rather noticeably. The general turnover in international missile-and-space industry programs for the period 1994–2001 exceeded four billion US dollars. Rather a large portion of this sum came from the use of Russian launchers in the international markets. One of these launchers is the 'Proton' system.[10] Some enterprises in this area have a very large share of their activities in international programs. For example, in recent years the Khrunichev Center's share in such activities constituted from 80 to 94 per cent[11].

As of January 2002, Rosaviakosmos had inter-governmental contracts with 18 countries, including the US, Japan, China, India, Bulgaria, Brazil, Argentina, and with the member-states of the European Space Agency (ESA). According to a statement by the General Director of Rosaviakosmos, Yuri Koptev, that company signed agreements with the space agencies of 19 states and with the ESA.[12] Successful cooperation with big foreign companies, international consortiums and international organizations also has a place. The Yuri Gagarin Center for Cosmonaut Training is successfully working in the field of preparing astronauts and cosmonauts for multi-national flights.

The organizational forms of this cooperation are becoming more diverse and more flexible. Thus, such forms include:

- inter-governmental agreements (such as the agreement on International Space Station of 29 January 1998);[13]
- inter-agency agreements (such as several agreements between Rosaviakosmos and NASA);
- joint ventures with foreign companies (such as the joint venture between the US company Pratt & Whitney and Russia's 'Energomash' to produce RD-180 engines);
- contracts on R&D and delivery of space techniques (the contract between the Russian design bureau HA and the US Aerojet Company on the research, development and construction of an engine based on the RD-0120);
- agreements and contracts on services that use space systems (the contract of the Russian design bureau 'Polyot' with the US and Sweden for the launch of FAISAT and ASTRID satellites);
- agreements for joint exchange by space services (the agreements on joint exchange of meteorological information within the framework of the World Meteorological Organization, and the agreement on joint space-based search and the KOSPAS-CAPCAT system).

There are also strategic partnerships between companies and space agencies, as between the West European company EADS and the

Russian Rosaviakosmos (the agreement was signed in December 2000).

One should stress that the intensive development of Russia's international cooperation in space, primarily with European partners, can also play an important role in expanding Russian cooperation with the US in this field.

As already mentioned above, given the dramatic reduction of state support to the Russian space industry, Russia's primary motivation for cooperation in outer space is now the survival of this industry, and preserving its production capabilities, workforce and technologies. Most recently this motivation has shifted to the need for integration into the world of cosmonautics, for access to modern technologies, for modernizing production facilities and seeing that they meet international standards. The role of economic motivation is also increasing, since it stimulates the necessary competitiveness of the Russian space industry in world markets.

At the same time, the motivations for international cooperation far exceed the framework of financial interests. Experience gained from past years of cooperation at the level of the laboratories demonstrates that professional links and involvement of space industry representatives in the world of scientific, technical and industrial communities are all very important, though less visible. This process is becoming a more and more current issue given globalization and integration. Owing to many factors – including sharply increased rates in the flow of scientific and technical knowledge, ideas, persons, resources, and their orientation toward joint work from the standpoint of financial resources and high-tech research; production in the field of space exploration; and the development of a commercial market – we can now speak about the process of creating a global scientific and technical base for the space industry. The capability of working with such a base is becoming an increasingly important factor for effective space activities. It is quite natural that the forms and methods for working with this base, which is still under construction, demand detailed and forward-looking assessments from the point of view of non-proliferation and security in general.

PROSPECTS FOR COOPERATION IN THE ABM ARENA

The issue of possible US-Russian cooperation in ballistic-missile defense is not a new one. This idea was among the first 'initiatives' of President Boris Yeltsin in January 1992 just after the collapse of the Soviet Union. But even earlier, during the Soviet-American Defense and Space Talks (which were a part of the more comprehensive START-1 negotiations) in the late 1980s and early 1990s, the US side tried to investigate the Soviet reaction to a possible transition to a strategic regime based not only on offensive nuclear weapons (and the concept of mutual assured destruction), but also on strategic defense. In Geneva the US delegation officially proposed discussing such a model by putting forward a draft of an agreement that called for such a transition to a defensive model 'based on cooperation' between the two states. That document, according to the US proposal, could replace the ABM Treaty of 1972. Despite pressure from the US side, the Soviet delegation refused to discuss such an idea or even ask and answer corresponding questions concerning the document, which was no big surprise to the American side, although it produced some disappointment against the background of the successes achieved at all the other US-Soviet talks.

The proposal of Russia in January 1992 looked more promising. In any case, both countries took concrete steps toward its further development and implementation. A working group was established (the Ross-Mamedov group), which met several times on this problem between 1992 and 1994. Nevertheless, this attempt never moved beyond general discussions, in the course of which the parties failed to achieve any common understanding on even the main principles of the development and use of a joint ABM system. However, in spite of the lack of success in this field, issues of US-Russian cooperation in the ABM arena are still on the agenda in the relations between the two countries.

This cooperation is very important not only from the point of view of the prospects for bilateral US-Russian relations, but also from the standpoint of international relations in general, since these questions are directly linked to the problems of national and international security. That is why the cooperation between Russia and the US in the ABM field should be a part of the broader substance of security cooperation. It is practically impossible to create new mechanisms of strategic stability in the twenty-first century.

ABM cooperation means cooperation in advanced and critically important technologies, many of which are dual-purpose. Cooperation in high-tech sectors of the economy is receiving more and more attention and development in the 'globalized' world. It often demands non-traditional approaches and decisions within a broad spectrum of interrelations and cooperation that include 'sensitive' technologies.

ABM cooperation will demand, among other things, stable US-Russian relations throughout the entire period of the development and construction of this system. But this will depend on many factors, including the success of democratic reforms in Russia, the effectiveness of the struggle against international terrorism, the results of military reform in Russia, and much more. In the view of a number of foreign experts, it will take not less then ten years to build a base for real and close Russian cooperation with Western countries in the area of military security.[14]

In this connection it is absolutely obvious that the parties need to develop and implement a new model of an inter-state relations and cooperation, including cooperation in outer space. A number of conditions must be met in order to make this model 'workable': a joint (equal) vision of the prospects for space exploration; common strategic perspectives in this (and other) security fields; a high level of transparency; 'liberalization' of the export of high technology and high-tech manufacturing in the space industry; removal of all discriminatory obstacles in US-Russian relations, including limitations on technology transfers. In addition, the parties need to 'institutionalize' Russian-American relations in this sphere. This means that the US and Russia need mechanisms for joint decision-making, resolving possible differences, preventing 'surprises' in space and, in general to establish a system capable of regulating all aspects of US-Russian cooperation in all the areas of their interrelations. In this regard, one of the important problems is the development of an effective mechanism for defining mutually beneficial conditions and structures for financing the joint projects and programs.

In our view, only after these conditions are met will the US and Russia be able to cooperate effectively in the ABM arena and in outer space in general. For now it is premature to expect such cooperation in the near future. But in the event that the parties clearly understand the situation and are willing to overcome the existing difficulties, one may say that the prospects are open.

CONCLUSION

Space, for many very understandable reasons, is the most realistic arena in which Russia and the US could try to overcome the historical obstacles in the path of promoting world security and strategic stability through cooperation in practically all current and prospective areas. Joint responsibility on the part of Russia and the US in this field could help solve many problems that the two countries face in the new century.

Cooperation between Russia and the US can play the central role in solving the task of global monitoring of outer space using national information assets, including early-warning satellites and ground-based ABM systems. Data exchange on space objects, the environment and other matters, can also contribute to strategic stability and international security.

Cooperation in the field of space control could help to work out a legal basis for international inspections of all space systems to be launched into orbit, as well as for international data exchange on hostile activities against these systems and their elements.

However, in order to move toward broad and successful US-Russian cooperation (to which, in principle, there are no serious alternatives) that is both stable and forward-looking, not only must the parties choose the optimal nature of their behavior, they must also create a new model of inter-governmental links. The basis of such a model must be the agreed-upon joint responsibility of the two states for global peace and stability, and for the character, ways and the consequences of the development of international space activities.

Regarding US-Russian cooperation in the ABM sphere, it is too early to speak of some large-scale program in this field. But that conclusion does not exclude the possibility of stable movement toward the development of a new international security system, with the participation not only of the two 'great space states', but also of other interested parties that are ready to share the responsibility for creating a new world order. Such cooperation would raise the general level of security relations and could become a decisive limiting factor against an arms race in outer space. It would also stimulate the process of developing a positive strategy for space exploration.

NOTES

1. We should also take into account the reduction of the gross domestic product itself during this period.
2. 'Russia's Space Program', *Aerokosmicheskiy Kurier* 1, 2000, p.13.
3. These figures were presented by the General Director of Rosaviakosmos, Yuri Koptev, during his testimony in the State Duma on 13 July 2001.

4. Sources: Hearings on Space in the State Duma on 14 Sept. 2000; *Novosti Kosmonavtiki* (Space News) 3 (2001) p.7.
5. Interview with Steven Redmaker, *Nezavisimoye Voennoye Obozreniye* (Independent Military Review) 10 (2003) p.2.
6. Within the framework of this commission, a Committee on Space worked very successfully alongside the committees on nuclear energy, science and technology, and others.
7. PAROS – Prevention of an Arms Race in Outer Space.
8. We should mention that no official decision has yet been taken on these issues.
9. 'Cosmonautics and the Problems of Civilization in the 21st Century', *New Technologies*, Vol. 21, Moscow, 2002, p.238.
10. *Aerokosmicheskiy Kurier* 1 (2002) p.10.
11. *Novosti Kosmonavtiki* 2 (2003).
12. *Aerokosmicheskiy Kurier* 1 (2002) p.9.
13. On 12 Dec. 1993, by special order, the Russian government expressed its agreement to participate in this program.
14. See, for example, M.Dihl (Germany), 'Russia and NATO Correlate Military Reforms', *Nezavisimoye Voennoye Obozreniye* 22 (2003) p.4.

The Anti-Oligarchy Campaign and its Implications for Russia's Security

VITALY SHLYKOV

The author examines the cross forces at play inside Russia between the government and the oligarchs. Why the crackdown on the oligarchy? Various prevailing theories are offered. Among them, perhaps this crackdown was a tactical campaign decision with "guaranteed voter appeal calculated to ensure a first-round victory for Putin." Or perhaps Khodorkovsky broke a tacit pact reached in 2000 with Putin, in which the oligarchs promised to stay out of politics and Putin agreed not to challenge the source of their wealth. The author notes that, "...businessmen are one of the few forces capable of resisting the onset of a new authoritarianism."

On 2 September 2003 President Vladimir Putin announced the official start of the parliamentary election campaign by setting 7 December as the date for the voting. But the campaign had actually begun two months earlier with the 2 July arrest of Platon Lebedev, director of Group Menatep and a major Yukos shareholder. Not only was Lebedev arrested, but Yukos' CEO, Mikhail Khodorkovsky, and his right-hand, Leonid Nevzlin, were called into the Prosecutor General's Office for questioning. Since then it has become clear that the main slogan for the election campaign will be 'Down with the oligarchs!'.

At first glance, Khodorkovsky was not the best possible target for such harsh treatment. He and Yukos are now the darlings of the Western media and investment community. Khodorkovsky is a frequent and warmly welcomed visitor in Washington, where he launched his Open Russia Foundation last year at the Library of

---

[Note: This article was written shortly before the arrest in Russia of Yukos oil magnate Mihail Khodorkovsky.]

Congress. The Foundation's board of trustees includes Lord Jacob Rothschild, Henry Kissinger and former US Ambassador to the Soviet Union, Arthur Hartman. The foundation awards grants to academic institutions and other non-profit organizations, while promoting Russian art in the West.

According to *Fortune* magazine's latest ratings of the top 500 earners, in 2002 Yukos was placed first in return on capital investments, which is defined as ratio of profits over assets (21.2 per cent), and ranked second (after Wyeth) in profit margins, which equaled 28 per cent. On 2 July the market capitalization of Yukos reached its peak of \$32.5 billion, the highest of any Russian company. And on that very day, after the market's close, Platon Lebedev, the director of Group Menatep, which is the majority shareholder in Yukos, was hauled out of a hospital in handcuffs on suspicion of embezzlement, dating back to 1994. According to the statement released by the Prosecutor General's Office, Lebedev is suspected of defrauding the state of more than \$280 million by illegally appropriating a stake in the Apatit joint stock company.

Apatit's story is typical of the shady privatization deals of the mid-1990s. It started in 1994 when an obscure firm called Volna bought a 20 per cent stake in Apatit, a Kirovsk/Murmansk-based fertilizer producer, for \$225,000 and a promise to invest the equivalent of \$280 million. The Murmansk regional government soon took Volna – which is widely believed to be owned by Khodorkovsky and Lebedev's industrial empire – to court for not making good on the \$280 million pledge. The region won its lawsuit in 1996, but by that time the 20 per cent stake had been resold to other firms.

The investigation was opened after State Duma Deputy Vladimir Yudin alerted law-enforcement agencies about the alleged embezzlement of Apatit shares. Yudin, a member of the pro-Kremlin Fatherland–All Russia faction, is deputy chairman of the Duma's economic policy committee. The case is being investigated as a fraud. If convicted, Lebedev could be sentenced to up to ten years in prison.

Lebedev, 46, was included in *Forbes* magazine's list of the world's billionaires this year for the first time. The magazine estimated his wealth at \$1 billion. Group Menatep, which he heads, is a Gibraltar-registered international holding company whose areas of activities are oil and gas, mineral fertilizers, banking and finance, telecommunications and portfolio investments. The group controls a 61 per cent share in Yukos.

On the same day that Lebedev was taken into custody, yet another Yukos arrest was announced, this one of a more criminal nature. Alexei Pichugin, the head of one of Yukos' powerful and notoriously thorough 'economic security' departments, was charged with the double murder of a husband and wife from Tambov, though it is unclear whether their bodies were ever found.

On 18 July the Prosecutor General's Office said that it had opened four new investigations into Yukos. All of them involve murder or attempted murder in 1998. A source at the prosecutor's office stated that these cases share a common link through 'property disputes between the victims' official and private entities and the Yukos oil company'. Prosecutors said that they are investigating whether Yukos played a part in the 26 June 1998 murder of Vladimir Petukhov, the mayor of Yukos' production capital, Nefteyugansk, in the Tyumen region. Petukhov had been leading a public campaign against Yukos over tax arrears, and many Nefteyugansk residents blamed the oil company for his death – which incidentally occurred on Khodorkovsky's 35th birthday.

Investigators also said they were trying to establish a link between Yukos and the attempted murder of Yevgeny Rybin, an executive of the Austrian-based oil company East Petroleum, in November 1998. Yukos acquired East Petroleum that year. The third investigation is into the October 1998 murder of Alexander Berlyand, the general director of Tomsk-Neft-Vostok Ltd., a trading partner of East Petroleum before its acquisition by Yukos. The fourth involves the December 1998 murder of a Nefteyugansk businessman identified by the prosecutors only as N. Filippov. With these four new cases, the Prosecutor General's Office has opened a total of seven investigations into Yukos. The seventh is an allegation of tax evasion.

At this stage it is difficult to say whether there is any substance behind the charges against either Yukos or its executives. However, what is pretty clear is that the arrests and investigations can be interpreted as an open attack by the Kremlin on Yukos founder and CEO, Mikhail Khodorkovsky. The accusations certainly fall on fertile soil. Back in the late 1990s when he had minority investors locked out of shareholders meetings, Khodorkovsky was seen as the embodiment of what had gone wrong in the country's transition to oligarchic capitalism. Questions were asked about how he parlayed his Communist Youth (Komsomol) connections in the early 1990s into the rights to handle billions of dollars worth of government accounts. Observers also wondered how he managed to acquire the bulk of Yukos, a company now worth from $20–$30 billion, for a mere $159 million in 1995.

The attack against Yukos was done with deliberate flamboyance. On 11 July about two dozen prosecutors and police, accompanied by armed men in masks, raided the Yukos archives and spent 17 hours going through the oil company's documents. When the investigators arrived, the company guards were told to lie face down on the floor. Later the prosecutor's office said guns and eavesdropping equipment were found during the search. Illegal weapons possession is one of the simplest charges to bring against a suspect, and conviction can lead to prison terms. Lebedev himself is being held in Lefortovo prison, which belonged to the KGB in Soviet times and is now run by the FSB. This institution is specifically reserved for people accused of terrorism, spying, treason and other political crimes. A businessman accused of theft is not sent to Lefortovo without a cause.

The Yukos affair has sent shudders through the Russian stock market, knocking more than $25 billion off its value as concerns mounted that the affair could herald a large-scale attack on Russia's fragile property rights. At first only Yukos, which lost several billion dollars in market capitalization after Lebedev's arrest, was seriously hit. The assault on 11 July cost the oil company another $1.9 billion, as its stock plummeted to $11.65 from its all-time high of $14.05 on 25 June. On 16 July the panic finally struck the rest of the market. The RTS index plummeted more than five per cent – the biggest one-day drop since the dark ages of post-crisis December 1998. Sibneft, the oil major with which Yukos was due to merge, fell almost ten per cent, while Unified Energy Systems (UES) dropped nearly eight per cent, and Gasprom lost more than five per cent. Yukos shares declined another seven per cent. In all, by that day, Yukos had lost almost $7 billion.

The 16 July market meltdown resulted from the lack of any clear sign that the conflict was going to end, an increasing realization among investors that the results of Russia's corrupt privatizations could still be up for grabs and from Khodorkovsky's apparent willingness to take on the Kremlin.

Khodorkovsky returned on that day from the US with a loud warning that the attack on his company could ruin the whole investment climate in Russia. In an unexpected show of defiance toward the Kremlin, Khodorkovsky told journalists at the airport that the Yukos case could unleash a new wave of capital flight. His talk about capital flight was construed by the market as a signal that he may be thinking about taking money out of the country. Some experts even say that the 16 July stock market decline was driven partially by Yukos-linked companies selling out. As one expert said, it is in Khodorkovsky's interest to create as much market fear as he can. 'It's as if Khodorkovsky's throwing a tantrum and saying, "if you don't let me do what I want, I'm going to bring everything down with me"', said the expert. More than that, Khodorkovsky is openly raising the political stakes in his fight against the snowballing investigations into his company, warning that the state risks turning back the clock to totalitarianism. 'For me, the situation is clear – the law-enforcement organizations decided that this was the best moment to show they could come to power', Khodorkovsky said in a television interview broadcast on 20 July. 'Today we must definitely decide whether our country's future will be totalitarian. If we hold strong, this will be resolved once and for all. However, there is a risk that we will once again return to this stagnant swamp.'

Khodorkovsky took this defiant stance despite the attitude of the market. Even some of the oligarchs were obviously expecting him to keep quiet and let the whole thing just die down. Typical in this respect is the attitude of one of the most prominent oligarchs, Vladimir Potanin, who openly admitted 'past mistakes', committed in the process of privatization and promised to make amends. Speaking at the first forum of the pro-Kremlin party 'United Russia' he said:

Just as you in politics struggle for the voices of the electorate, we entrepreneurs attempt to restore the trust of the people in our activities. To a great extent, this trust was lost due to the mistakes we made in the process of the initial accumulation of capital. We are in debt to society. To achieve our purposes we need to recover that trust. Please help us, and together we will tackle the tasks put before us by the President.

It is hardly surprising that after this public oath of allegiance to the Kremlin the stock of Potanin's Norilsk Nickel fared better during the market's meltdown than almost anybody else's.

One possible reason for Khodorkovsky's defiance is that he hopes to rally around himself powerful allies both inside and outside

Russia. One such ally is quite obvious. It is the so-called 'Family' around Yeltsin. Two of its most prominent members, Roman Abramovich and Oleg Deripaska, must also feel threatened by the same enemy who has attacked Yukos. Speculation is mounting that Roman Abramovich, Russia's second-richest man with an estimated fortune of $5.7 billion, might be preparing to pull out of the country altogether. Citing anonymous sources, two leading Moscow dailies, *Kommersant* and *Gazeta*, both reported on 11 July that the Siberian oil tycoon is in talks to sell his half of RusAl. One interested buyer, according to the papers, is Oleg Deripaska, who owns the other half of RusAl. *Gazeta* also mentioned Viktor Vekselberg, who, in addition to [his holding company] SUAL, controls a large chunk of Tyumen Oil Company (TNK), for which he is set to receive part of the $6 billion that BP has agreed to pay to merge its Russian operations with TNK. Neither Millhouse Capital, the holding company that manages Abramovich's assets, nor RusAl, would comment on what they called market rumors. But a source close to Deripaska's holding company, Base Element, said that Abramovich and Deripaska, when they created RusAl, agreed to freeze any asset sales for three years, a time limit that has just expired.

The possibility of an assault on Abramovich looks quite logical if the Kremlin is really out to cut Khodorkovsky down to size – Yukos and Abramovich's Sibneft are trying to finalize a merger that would create Russia's first-tier global oil company. The Kremlin reportedly does not favor having such a huge and influential company uncontrolled by the state. If these reports are true, the sale of Abramovich's RusAl stake would be the latest in a string of sell-offs. In March, he sold his 26 per cent stake in the national airline, Aeroflot, for an estimated $130 million. A month later, the Yukos-Sibneft merger was announced. If concluded, it would net Abramovich the lion's share of the $3 billion in cash Yukos will pay to take over its smaller rival. Abramovich is also seeking to sell his 37.5 per cent stake in Deripaska's Ruspromavto holding, which includes Russia's number two automaker, GAZ. But it is not only the merger with Yukos that makes Abramovich an obvious next target for attack. His recent $230 million playboy-style splurge on the British soccer club Chelsea has ruffled some influential feathers back home. The Audit Chamber chief and former prime minister Sergei Stepashin, for example, has accused Sibneft of dodging $300 million in taxes, which, Stepashin suggested, was used to buy Chelsea. Already raids by men in masks have been conducted in the offices of Sibneft. By an ominous coincidence Lebedev was arrested on Wednesday, 2 July, the same very day Abramovich announced that he was buying Chelsea.

Oleg Deripaska, too, seems to be getting into the whirlpool of an anti-oligarchy campaign. On 14 July the Prosecutor General's Office announced that it has reopened a criminal investigation into how Deripaska's Base Element got control of insurance giant Ingosstrakh from entrepreneur Andrei Andreyev. The latter says that he is the legal owner of majority stakes in Ingosstrakh, controlled now by Base Element, as well as Avtobank and dozens of other companies that were sold in September 2001 – without his consent, he says. Avtobank executive Natalia Rayevskaya and one Rodion Gamzayev, about whom little is known, signed the agreement allowing the sale, while David Davidovich, a board member of RusAl, signed the agreement on the buyer's behalf. Andreyev, who has lately been making frequent appearances on television, insists that both co-owners of RusAl, Deripaska and Abramovich, knew perfectly well that they were buying stolen property.

In April of 2002, the assets in question, including 84 per cent of Ingosstrakh and 65 per cent of Avtobank, were frozen by authorities, pending a court decision on rightful ownership. But in June of that year the shares were unfrozen, and Base Element and its partners began trading the shares that Andreyev says are his. Now the Prosecutor General's Office says that the decision to close the case was made 'unobjectively' by investigators from the Interior Ministry, where the prosecutor's protests were ignored.

There are many theories making the rounds in Moscow as to why Yukos has been attacked.

Theory 1: President Vladimir Putin ordered the crackdown as part of an election campaign strategy based on doing battle with the oligarchs. This was a tactical decision with guaranteed voter appeal calculated to ensure a first-round victory for Putin.

Theory 2: A few years ago the security services went after Vladimir Potanin, demanding that he pay the government $140 million for what they called the undervalued privatization of Norilsk Nickel. Rumor has it that they secretly asked for money and that Potanin agreed. If he had not, some of his people would now be behind bars. Then they went after Yukos, again with their hands out. But Khodorkovsky would not pay.

Theory 3: Over the past month, Khodorkovsky has branched out into politics. He has openly said that he is funding the Union of Right(ist) Forces and Yabloko parties, and that another member of the Yukos board is funding the Communists. The rumor has been that he wants to make sure he can count on the support of up to half of the State Duma deputies who are to be elected in December. Boris Nemtsov, leader of the Union of Right(ist) Forces faction in the Duma, agrees that it was Khodorkovsky's political activities that motivated the case against Lebedev. 'This is revenge for Yukos management's intention to increase its presence in the political process', he said. By getting involved in politics, analysts point out, Khodorkovsky broke the tacit pact reached in 2000 with Putin, in which the oligarchs promised to stay out of politics and Putin agreed not to challenge the source of their wealth.

According to many analysts, Yukos has Khodorkovsky's only thinly veiled political ambitions to thank for its predicament. Despite many reports that he might be preparing for presidential elections sometime in the future, he so far has given no clear answer to direct questions on whether he may run for the presidency.

Theory 4: Khodorkovsky is not the only, or even the most important, target. The case against Yukos is only the beginning of an attack by former KGB members who moved into the Kremlin with Putin and are opposed to the old oligarchic elite, including Abramovich, Deripaska, Friedman, *et al.*, who made their fortunes and wielded immense political influence in the Yeltsin era.

Theory 5: The affair is connected to rumors of a coming merger between Yukos and Exxon or Shell, a move that would create the world's largest oil company, bringing substantial foreign capital and foreign influence into Russia and make Khodorkovsky immensely rich and virtually untouchable. The attack is also intended to derail Yukos' merger with Sibneft later this year in a complex cash and equity transaction, valued by analysts at up to $15 billion, which would make Yukos the country's biggest oil producer. At present Yukos produces 1.6 million bbl per day of oil. Its output would rise to 2.3 million bbl per day after it acquires Sibneft.

Other theories proffer more complicated explanations, involving a power struggle in the Kremlin between those who support the idea that Russia should continue moving toward a liberal society, versus members of the old security services who want to turn back the clock.

Khodorkovsky himself has made no secret of his belief that the pressure being put on his oil company is the result of a Kremlin power struggle. 'My opinion is', he says, 'that we are seeing here the beginning of a fight between various branches of the sphere around Vladimir Vladimirovich Putin.'

Most analysts agree that there is a clash within the Kremlin and that nobody knows which side Putin is going to come out on. Putin himself has so far made no statement on the situation in Yukos or on his policy toward past privatization. He has issued conflicting signals, saying that economic crimes must be fought but not by using 'arm-twisting and jail cells'. He has not mentioned Yukos directly, but Arkady Volsky, president of the Russian Union of Industrialist and Entrepreneurs (RSPP), the main lobbying group for Russia's oligarchs, informed the media after meeting with President Putin on 16 July that Putin told him that he would not interfere in the case.

But, just as it is almost unthinkable that a move against an oligarch on this scale could be made without the president's sanction (or at least a tacit nod), it is exceedingly unlikely that the whole thing will simply blow over without a direct public intervention by him. If the plan was to deliver a 'surgical strike' against Khodorkovsky for overstepping the mark politically and to flash a warning to the rest of the business elite in the run-up to the elections, without undermining political stability, things seem to have gone obviously awry.

There is clearly concern in many quarters, including the Kremlin, that what is essentially an intra-elite conflict could spill over and impact the body politic with unpredictable consequences.

Commenting on the Yukos saga, presidential economic advisor Andrey Illarionov came out on 14 July with the first strong statement from someone in the presidential administration on the dangers of revisiting privatization, even going so far as to evoke the specter of civil war. Weighing in on the Yukos affair, Illarionov came out on the side of business and issued the gravest warning yet of the dangers of undoing the privatization deals of the mid-1990s. 'If we start now to revisit privatization, it will not be easy to stop the process, and it is not inconceivable that such action will lead to a new civil war', he said on Ekho Moskvy radio. 'It is not difficult to open a Pandora's box, but it will be very difficult to close it', he added.

The business elite, meanwhile, has been at the forefront of raising the specter of re-nationalization and civil war, presumably in order to put pressure on Putin to take a firm stance. On 17 July, RSSP, OPORA (an association of small businesses), '*Delovaya Rossiya*' (an organization uniting mid-size business) and the Commission on Human Rights under President Putin, held a forum titled 'Power, Business and Human Rights'. The forum concluded that the present situation in Russia has all the characteristics of a systemic crisis, and that what is happening to Yukos is just a visible part of a war started by both society and the authorities against the business community. As proof, the forum participants cited numerous cases of deprivatization in the regions, where governors and mayors take away from owners their formerly privatized property using police and prosecutors as tools for reprivatization.

In the view of the participants, 75 per cent of the population support repressive measures against the oligarchs and a review of the former privatization processes, whereas hundreds of thousands of employees of the security services of the big corporations are ready to defend their places of work and their relatively high salaries with arms in hand. In this situation, the forum participants note, a premonition of civil war no longer seems like paranoia.

In a letter published on 22 July, without naming Yukos, leaders of the three business associations mentioned above, as well as several prominent rights activists, stated that 'arbitrariness and intimidation' by the authorities threaten the nation's stability. Its authors proposed that the government sign a pact with the business community that would guarantee the irreversibility of privatization results. Businesses, in turn, would pledge to help combat corruption and do more to solve social problems.

Andrey Illarionov, who is known for speaking his own mind without necessarily reflecting Putin's views, says that in his opinion it would be best to decide on a date before which privatizations deals would not be revisited. He means it would be better to start afresh, with everyone held in accordance with the law from that point on. 'It is because either you have to review all the deals, which will just lead us to a national catastrophe and this is no exaggeration, or if you don't review all the deals, then it is an example of selective approach, of double standards', he says.

Illarionov's proposal to draw a line in the sand and effectively declare an amnesty (in all but name) on all privatization prior to a certain date seems an eminently sensible one under the circumstances. It is increasingly clear that the deal that President Putin struck with the oligarchs three years ago – that they could keep their ill-gotten gains, as long as they became good corporate citizens and did not interfere directly in politics – has fallen apart. And it is no surprise, as there were never any hard-and-fast rules, and the deal was always open to interpretation.

But at the same time, one cannot help feeling that the current state of instability and insecure property rights really suits the Kremlin. The threat of reviewing privatization is a powerful instrument for ensuring the loyalty of big business, and the oligarchs' insecurity makes them a prime target for shakedowns of one sort or another.

The state's schizophrenia is captured in the different reactions of the government and the Kremlin to the prosecutor's hyperactivity around Yukos. Members of the government, including Prime Minister Mikhail Kasyanov, were fairly quick to disapprove of the prosecutors' actions and to seek to dispel the business community's fears. The presidential administration, on the other hand, has been in no hurry to comment one way or the other. But its real sentiment was probably expressed by Gleb Pavlovsky, considered to be the Kremlin's unofficial main ideologist. In his opinion, it is impossible to declare an amnesty on the previous privatizations, because the process of privatization has not been concluded. Besides, in his view, private property in Russia simply does not yet exist.

At the heart of the scandal around Yukos is a conflict between the Yeltsin and Putin elites. President Boris Yeltsin used to reshuffle personnel so frequently that officials were prepared for dismissal at any moment. He brought to the pinnacle of power people who had no prior experience in government service or business practice. The secretive President Vladimir Putin acts quietly and almost imperceptibly, but in the three years of his presidency the Russian elite has changed fundamentally. The corridors of power have swelled with people from a military, law-enforcement or security-service background. It is no big secret that Putin trusts those he has worked with and people from St Petersburg. But the extent to which the authorities have become militarized only really becomes apparent on close study. Between 2001 and 2003 the Institute of Sociology of the Russian Academy of Sciences conducted research on the Putin elite. More than 3,500 biographies have been analyzed. They include government members, senior presidential administration personnel, deputies of both chambers of the Federal Assembly, the regional elite and major businessmen.

The results of the study make interesting reading. It is the staffs of the presidential envoys in the seven federal districts, established by Putin, that have experienced the most precipitous invasion of military personnel (up to 70 per cent of the total). And whereas the heads of the local branches of the FSB, Interior Ministry, Tax Police and the Prosecutor's Office used to be under the de facto control of the governors, that control is now exercised by the presidential envoys. In each federal district, security councils have been set up that include the regional heads of law enforcement, military and intelligence agencies. This has stripped the regional elite of a serious support base.

However, serious changes have occurred at the regional level, as well. The number of people with a military or security background has more than doubled over the past three years. A few years ago, affiliation with the security services was considered a big minus for gubernatorial hopefuls. The situation changed after 2000, and it is now fashionable to have a military or, in particular, a security background. These days that is interpreted as an indication that the candidate has Kremlin backing.

But no less interesting is the fact that more people with a military or security background are now working in economic ministries. Thus, among the deputy ministers appointed between 2000 and 2003, 35 per cent come from such a background. Moreover, the majority of them come from various departments of the FSB and have retained their status as 'active reserve officers'. This status normally means that an officer is seconded to another agency, but preserves his FSB salary and privileges, and is obliged to report not only to his minister, but also to the FSB. The greatest concentration of 'military' deputy ministers can be found in the Economic Development and Trade Ministry, the Ministry of Science, Industry and Technology, the Communications Ministry, the Press Ministry and the Justice Ministry.

In general, over the three years of Putin's presidency, the elite has become more militarized and less intellectual. Whereas in the early 1990s the elite's strategic core consisted mainly of economists, under Putin military men and security officers have gained the upper hand in shaping national strategy. This has altered the state's priorities with issues of security, military reform and the country's geopolitical place in the world coming very much to the fore.

It is true that Putin's military and security cohort has passed through the school of democratization, and in many cases worked in the private sector or abroad. Their inbred authoritarianism has undergone modernization and transformation. The impulse to control everything and everyone has been circumscribed by the law, the norms of Western living standards and an eye to how the international community will react. Control, in some cases, takes on covert forms, such as planting Kremlin commissars in the regions, using administrative resources to swing elections, taking the lead in creating institutions of civil society, and planting agents of influence in business and the media. This kind of organization is stable, especially as it is held together by patriotic ideology and the corporate spirit inculcated in security-service officers.

But the oligarchs, for their part, have not been idle, either. Another prominent feature of the Putin administration has been the number of big business protégés assuming positions of power. In the past three years, according to the Institute of Sociology, their number has grown sevenfold. This process began under Yeltsin and, in contrast to the influx of military men, is not directly linked to the president's personnel preferences. Many oligarchs, unlike Khodorkovsky, have come a long way from naive attempts to get involved in politics themselves to the development of entire networks of representatives at every level of government. At the moment, their representatives occupy 16 per cent of the country's top leadership positions, 17 per cent of the Federal Assembly and five per cent of government positions. Given that there is no real separation of powers in Russia and that the Kremlin is expanding control to all areas of public life, and in the absence of a strong political opposition, businessmen are one of the few forces capable of resisting the onset of a new authoritarianism. Recent history has handed Russian big business the unusual role of providing some form of checks and balances.

In a confrontation with the secret services, the oligarchs look like an obvious underdog. Actually, they are a politician's dream. Their fortunes rest on corrupt foundations and their political clout rests on the feebleness of the elected government. Every constituency, from nationalists to foreigners, from neo-conservatives to communists, from the security services to the military and the defense-industrial complex agree on the need to rein them in.

Unnoticed by most Russian political observers, Putin seems to have already given a signal for an all-out attack on the oligarchy.

The signal is hidden in the last presidential address to parliament delivered on 16 May. In it Putin enumerates three main strategic tasks (they've already been dubbed 'the Putin triad') facing Russia: doubling the country's GDP by 2010; modernizing the armed forces; and, overcoming poverty. In effect, by proclaiming these tasks Putin opened three wide corridors for attack on the oligarchs under the protective banner of fulfilling the presidential directives. The attack has already begun.

The main vote-getting part of the triad is obviously the war on poverty. The newly-built party, tentatively called '*Tovarishch*' ('Comrade') with Sergey Glaziev as its leader, has already made the war on poverty the focus of its election campaign. Glaziev promises to take away 90 per cent of the oil and rent, amounting, in his estimate, to \$20 to \$30 billion. This money, taken away from the oligarchs, would make it possible to increase the annual income of an average family of four by \$150.[1] As for doubling the GDP, it is being closely linked with military modernization. Most economists agree that this goal is unachievable with the present predominance in the Russian economy of the export-oriented raw materials sector, which comprises half of the national production. (In 2000 the energy sector comprised 30 per cent, other mining industries 20.4 per cent, the machine-building and metalworking sector 18.8 per cent and other processing industries 30.8 per cent of the industrial production.)[2] In an interview titled 'The Great Military Product – Only the High-tech Sector Can Fulfill the President's Task of Doubling the GDP', the president of Russia's largest private defense-industrial corporation, New Programs and Concepts, Boris Kouzyk, says:

The president has set the task of doubling the GDP over the next ten years. Only the high-tech industries can cope with this task. Today the world high-technology sector produces goods worth \$2.8 trillion a year, while the energy sector accounts for only \$560–570 billion. According to a forecast of the Institute for Economic Strategies, the high-technology complex will increase its production in the next ten years to \$9.3–9.5 trillion. It is clear that the energy sector, where the annual growth does not exceed 2.5% to 3.0% a year, cannot grow at a similar rate. And I think that the problem of increasing rent payments [by the producers of raw materials] is urgent. . . . Of course, those who will have to pay won't like the idea. But we must think about the interests of the state. In a situation when our federal budget only slightly exceeds that of New York City, there simply does not exist any other way out . . . I want to see Russia reliably protected. For this we need a high-technology army and first-class specialists. After we have examined all possible threats and the ways of dealing with them we have to sit down and count how much it would cost.

If it turns out that we need more money than the state can afford, we should go to the oligarchs and tell them: To defend the oil shelf, we need a navy of such and such a size. So in order to assure the security and strategic future of your business, we introduce rent payments to finance such and such an armaments programs.[3]

Putin's appeal to double the GDP and to modernize the military also strengthened the hand of those economists who view the defense-industrial complex as a locomotive for accelerating Russia's economic growth. The influential Russian economist and director of the Institute for Economic Forecasting of the Russian Academy of Sciences, Viktor Ivanter, writes, for example:

The president has set the ambitious task of doubling the country's GDP over a decade. What does that mean? As the export-oriented raw materials sector cannot grow more than 2% to 3% a year, the needed yearly 7% to 8% growth can be achieved only if the growth in the manufacturing industries is in the double digits. Is it realistic to maintain this kind of growth over at least a decade? My answer is yes. But only on the condition that we give up the late XIX-early XX century dogma of 'guns instead of butter'. In those days it was thought that a country can effectively develop either the defense or the civilian industry, but not both at the same time. In those days it was true, but now things are different. If we really want to develop high technologies, the state has to finance defense projects, especially those that belong to the real enclaves of the important technical and scientific breakthroughs. The high technologies embodied in the military goods produced with state money will be slowly flowing into the private-production sector on an absolutely commercial basis. To sum up, what is needed is large-scale defense procurement by the state. The money for defense is available. It is our budget surplus. Actually we do not know what to do with all that money. It should be spent on precisely defined and controllable projects in the defense-industrial complex. In this way we can kill two birds with one stone – developing high technologies and insuring the military might of the state.[4]

The link between the presidential goal of doubling the GDP and the defense-industrial interests is not coincidental, considering the real driving forces behind the anti-oligarchy campaign, which first broke into the open with the arrest of Platon Lebedev. Back then, Mikhail Khodorkovsky said that the arrest was the result of inter-clan fighting inside the Kremlin. Now, two months later, some of the participants of the infighting have decided to step forward from behind the scenes.

On 29 August, Gleb Pavlovsky, long known as one of Russia's most influential spin doctors (he was a key public-relations figure for Putin's 2000 election campaign), wrote for Kremlin chief of staff

Alexander Voloshin a memorandum, in which he accuses a group led by Mezhprombank founder Sergei Pugachev and high-ranking members of the presidential administration Viktor Ivanov and Igor Sechin of mounting 'a creeping coup' and creating a 'parallel center of power'. According to Pavlovsky, Pugachev's group is based on an economic clan consisting of the state-owned oil company Rosneft, Mezhprombank and parts of the state-controlled gas monopoly, Gazprom. Pavlovsky's report says that the group strives for 'a redistribution of property in its own favor and a mass change of elites on a federal and regional level'. This, if allowed to continue, will lead to Putin's becoming 'a hostage to the policies of the group' and a return to 'the instability that marked the end of the 1990s'.[5]

Pavlovsky says in his report that the Pugachev group is trying to pull many sectors of the economy into its orbit, including transportation, banking, oil and coal. In his opinion, its purpose is to build 'state-oriented capitalism' in which all owners would be completely loyal to the state. If owners were not loyal, he writes, they would be subjugated by force, as seen in the attack on Khodorkovsky. Under the plan, 'business itself would remain private, but the role of the state in running it should be high... there is a growing tendency for a redistribution of property in the interests of this group, which is hiding under the flag of state interests', the report says. 'In place of the destroyed oligarchic system, a new "*silovaya*" (strong-arm) oligarchy consisting of members of this group and their frontmen will take its place.' Pavlovsky claims that the group is trying to push Putin into supporting it by publicly complaining of his 'weakness' and 'indecision' in not breaking off ties with the Yeltsin 'Family' and the oligarchs and accusing him of turning into another Gorbachev. He also claims that the group is seeking to reorient the economy from its free-market base and create strong, state-owned monopolies in the most important sectors of the economy, redistribute resources and property, tighten its control over business, and turn the secret services into Putin's main power base.

There are signs that the Pugachev group is trying to get a firm foothold in the defense industry and turn it into its stronghold. And this is where possibly the first warning shots in the war between the *siloviki* and the oligarchs fell.

On 6 June 2003, Igor Klimov, acting general director of the Almaz-Antei holding, was shot dead outside his Moscow apartment building. On the same day Sergey Shchitko, commercial director of [the Almaz-Antei subsidiary –Trans.] RATEP, was killed by three gunshots to the head while sitting in a car outside a cafe in a Moscow suburb, where RATEP is located.

Klimov, who was appointed acting head of Almaz-Antei in February 2003, was charged with the task of merging close to 50 companies into a single giant concern that would virtually monopolize the nation's air defense industry. After his appointment he pledged to complete the formation of the concern by year's end and adjust its marketing policies to boost annual sales to $2 billion within the next five years.

The Almaz-Antei holding was formed in accordance with a presidential decree signed on 23 April 2002. As for RATEP, it is one of dozens of smaller companies that make up Almaz-Antei.

Settling business by way of contract killings is nothing unusual in Russia. What makes these two murders atypical is the personality of Igor Klimov. Prior to his joining Almaz-Antei, he served as an aide to Colonel General Viktor Ivanov, a former intelligence officer, a deputy head of the presidential administration and Vladimir Putin's personal friend from St Petersburg, whom the president appointed to head Almaz-Antei's board of directors. It is the same Viktor Ivanov whom Pavlovsky mentioned as a member of the Pugachev group. Ruling out some common crime, there exists the possibility, some experts point out, that somebody was sending a message to Viktor Ivanov or his group to stop the seizure of their property under the banner of setting up state-controlled monopolies by administrative means. Sergei Pugachev, who is heavily involved in the defense industry (he is the largest stockholder of Boris Kouzyk's New Programs and Concepts group) might be also one those who was getting the message.

In response to Pavlovsky's report, Sergei Pugachev issued a statement that the report contains 'a whole series of fabricated, insulting, knowingly untrue and slanderous accusations about me' and that what Pavlovsky wrote 'is of a criminal and illegal nature'.

Pavlovsky's and Pugachev's exchange of accusations is just one of a growing number of indications that neither side in the conflict is going to back down or seek a compromise. Both feuding parties are obviously trying to strengthen their positions and mobilize supporters for a possible all-out confrontation. A protégé of Viktor Ivanov's, state-security Major-General Vladislav Menshikov, was appointed at the end of August as the new general director of Almaz-Antei. Several days later Mikhail Khodorkovsky bought the influential weekly newspaper *Moskovskiye Novosti* and appointed former prominent television anchor Yevgeny Kiselyov as its editor-in-chief.

It is hard to say at this stage when an all-out conflict with all its implications for Russia's security will flare up. So far neither of the opposing parties seems to be sure whose side President Putin is on or is in the process of trying to force his hand.

The question is whether Putin will be able to steer between the Scylla of militocracy and secret police and the Charybdis of the oligarchy.

Of course, there is a third way for Russia in which, however, only few optimists believe. Russians continue to show an unprecedented amount of trust in their president. His approval ratings remain at 65 per cent on average. The population, which, according to polls, has little or no trust in the government and bureaucracy, seems infatuated with Putin. If he wishes to bring about change, he has nearly the whole population solidly behind him. With this mass support that a democratically elected leader elsewhere can only dream about, he could afford to challenge both the super-rich elite and the comfortably established security services, whose tentacles reach deep into all levels of politics and government.

So far Putin, despite some very brave noise, has proven incapable of taking on this true challenge. Instead, he has opted simply to trim the shrubbery of state structures in what could be termed a less potent form of *perestroika*. He has been blessed with rare fortune, and Russia has seen amazing economic windfalls in the past three years thanks to high oil prices. But Putin has not shown any tendency to capitalize on this by taking greater political and economic risks to bring about substantial democratic changes. Now with the scandal around Yukos, he has a rare opportunity to deal decisively with both sides in the conflict and steer Russia to a better future. In any case, it looks like an eventful period for Russia watchers around the globe.

NOTES

1. *Ekspert*, 1 Sept. 2003.
2. *Profil*, 1 Sept. 2003, p.27.
3. *Itogi*, 15 July 2003.
4. *Ekspert*, 21 July 2003. More on the theory of 'guns and butter', which the author attributes to me, can be found in Professor Steven Rosefielde's article 'Back to the Future? Prospects for Russia's Military Industrial Revival', *Orbis*, Summer 2002.
5. <http://www.polit.ru/docs/624242.html>.

The Soviet–Afghan War: A Superpower Mired in the Mountains

LESTER W. GRAU

The Soviet-Afghan War involved more than the Soviets and Mujahideen resistance. Afghan communists (the DRA) were involved in the immediate struggle and a large number of countries supplied the Mujahideen during this "Cold War" hot war. Their struggle and their lessons are outlined. The author does not usually write about footnotes, but he wrote this article during a trip to Iraq and lacked his reference library. Needless to say, he drew on his knowledge about the war and the knowledge he gained from noted authorities on the subject. These include Ali Jalali, Barnett Rubin, Riaz Khan, Mohammad Youssaf, Brace Amstutz, Artem Borovik, Aleksandr Lyakhovskiy, Aleksandr Mayorov, Scott McMichael, Makhmut Gareev, David Isby, Boris Gromov, Rasul Rais, and Louis Dupree.

Soaring mountains dominate Afghanistan and shape its culture, history, social structure, customs, politics and economy. Vast, trackless deserts, mighty rivers and lush cropland further define this remote country. Militarily, the operational key terrain is the limited road network that connects its cities in a giant ring with side roads to Pakistan, Iran, Turkmenistan, Uzbekistan and Tajikistan. There are only 24 kilometers of railroad in Afghanistan – and these are split into two unconnected segments – leftover spurs from the former Soviet Union's incursion. During the nineteenth and early twentieth centuries, many countries offered to build railroads in Afghanistan, but Afghanistan was bordered to the north by the Russian Empire, to the east by the British Empire and to the west by Persia, heir to the late Persian Empire. The rulers of Afghanistan noted that the armies of empire traveled on rail and no railroads were built in Afghanistan. Militarily, this was probably a wise choice, but it exacted a severe economic and political price. To this day, Afghanistan is one of the most poverty-stricken and isolated countries on the planet.

There are some eternal truths about Afghanistan.

First, it is a fragmented land in which a strong central government is an anomaly. Tribal chiefs and regional warlords exert considerable power and the central government requires extraordinary leadership to control and dominate its unruly regions. Rural Afghans think of themselves primarily in tribal and peer group (*qwam*) terms, not as Afghans. The one event that unites all Afghans in a common cause is foreign invasion. The central government's army has seldom been strong enough to repel external invasion, but the country's true combat power lies in the rural lands and remote mountains where warriors hold sway.

Second, combat in the mountainous regions is seasonal. In November, the snows fall, closing the mountain passes and forcing the people down into the valleys where they winter over. Little fighting occurs, except in the low desert regions. In March and April, the snows begin to melt and combatants begin to stir. May and June are excellent months for combat. July and August are too hot and the pace of combat slows. September and October are again excellent months for combat. And in November, the snows fall.

Third, combat in Afghanistan has a certain logic to it. Battles between Afghans are never fought 'to the knife' where one side attempts to annihilate the other completely. Rather, when it is apparent that one side is winning, the other side kicks out a rear guard and melts into the mountains. The rear guard in a distinct body take the bulk of the casualties. When foreigners invade Afghanistan, however, the Afghans are capable of annihilation combat. The British 'Army of the Indus' that perished between Kabul and Gandamak in 1842 and the British 'Burrows Brigade' that was wiped out at Maiwand in 1880 are two prime examples.

Fourth, personal loyalty is primarily to family, *qwam* (social, school or trade group) and tribe. Higher loyalty to cause and regional or national leaders is situational. Units may change sides in battle when the other side is winning. A common perception is that the other side is winning because it is God's will and one should not oppose God's will. Temporary truces and alliances are common. Loyalty can be rented, but the term length of the rental is uncertain.

BACKGROUND

The Afghanistan of the 1970s was a fairly liberal Islamic country. *Purdah* was rare in the cities and one saw more women in miniskirts than in *burqahs*. In Kabul, discos blared country and eastern music until early in the morning. Literacy rates were low, perhaps ten per cent. The power of the mullahs and imams was restricted to religious matters. Secular leaders controlled the country, provinces, districts, cities and villages. Tribal power was strong, but challenged by the increasing urbanization of the country. There was an inherent friction between the more liberal urban populace and the conservative rural community. Before he was deposed, the king was working to modernize and enlighten the country – an effort that did not always sit well with the rural and religious community.

Afghanistan is an ethnically diverse society with a Pashtu, Uzbek, Tajik, Hazara and Nuristani populace. The primary languages are Pashtun and Dari. Turkmen, Tajik, Uzbek and Baluch are also spoken. The country is overwhelmingly Islamic with the majority being Sunni. The Hazara are Shia and closely affiliated with neighboring Iran. The country has a strong Sufi tradition, but during the Soviet–Afghan War, Wahhabism and Deobandism made strong inroads due to substantial external financial contributions to the cause.

Afghanistan has a traditional warrior society and a strong sense of independence. Male children receive a firearm before their teens and learn to use it. Most men carry a weapon. Still, rifle marksmanship is not all that good, particularly since the introduction of the Kalashnikov assault rifle. Further, their weapons handling is casual and muzzles point everywhere – an unfortunate habit only partially alleviated by the fact that there is seldom a round in the weapon's chamber. The independent nature of the people means that they are reluctant to accept military discipline. They can be fierce warriors but indifferent soldiers.

The northern part of Afghanistan, bordering the Soviet Union, was a major agricultural area. The river valleys were also fertile and productive. Agriculture products were Afghanistan's major exports. Truckloads of melons, grapes, wheat, apples, nuts and even rice crossed the borders of Pakistan and Iran.

The Soviet Union had a long and fairly friendly relationship with its southern neighbor. Afghanistan was the first nation to recognize the Soviet Communist regime after the Bolshevik Revolution.

Modest amounts of Soviet aid, accompanied by Soviet advisers, entered Afghanistan in the 1920s and were a constant feature in Afghanistan during the next 50-plus years. One of the best country studies and military appreciations on Afghanistan was published in 1921 by Andrey E. Snesarev, a Tsarist and Soviet general who had toured the area extensively (and spoke 14 languages) [A.E. Snesarev. Afghanistan, Moscow: Gosydarstrennor izdatcl'Stro, 1921.]. In 1930, the Soviets briefly invaded northern Afghanistan in hot pursuit of a fleeing Uzbek leader.

Turkey and Germany also sought influence and advantage in Afghanistan. Turkish and German military advisers helped train the Afghan Army. During World War II, German Abwehr and Soviet NKVD agents conducted a deadly contest in Kabul. The Abwehr lost. The United States (US) belatedly tried for influence in Afghanistan following World War II. President Eisenhower even paid a brief visit to the country in 1956. Both the US and the Soviet Union contributed economic aid and embarked on a series of infrastructure development projects in the 1960s and 1970s. The Soviet Union built airfields and roads in the northern part of the country, including the world's highest traffic tunnel – the Salang tunnel – a marvel of engineering stretching two miles and allowing transit of the rugged Hindu Kush mountains. The Soviets also developed the Kabul river irrigation project south of Jalalabad. The US built roads in the south of the country and the Kandahar airfield as well as the extensive Helmand basin irrigation project. The Chinese were also competing – with an extensive irrigation system near Charikar. Thousands of Afghan officials, officers and students studied in the Soviet Union.

In July 1973, Prime Minister Daoud overthrew his cousin, the king, and set himself up as the President of Afghanistan. The shift from monarchy to a parliamentary system was not unopposed. Students dropped out of school and took to the mountains as guerrillas opposing the new president. They joined guerrillas who had started by opposing the reforms of the king. These isolated Mujahideen (holy warriors) would later become the basis for nationwide resistance.

In the 1970s, communism and nationalism were sweeping the planet. The West was in retreat as Vietnam, Laos, Cambodia, Angola, Mozambique and Ethiopia became communist. Revolutionary Iran threw the West out of the country, the Middle East was in chaos and Chile, Argentina and El Salvador were tottering on the brink of joining the communist camp. The future looked red and uninspired

US leadership did little to rally the West. The Soviet Union was clearly in ascendancy and Soviet military internationalists were in Cuba, Vietnam, Laos, Ethiopia, Angola, Mozambique, Congo, Egypt, Syria and Latin America. The Soviet Union was supporting revolutionary cells in West Germany, Italy, Spain, France and Japan and providing financial aid to Western communist parties. Communist espionage had thoroughly penetrated the West.

Daoud's regime did not last long. In April 1978, Daoud was overthrown by a communist coup engineered by army and air force officers who had studied in the Soviet Union. The emergent Democratic Republic of Afghanistan (DRA) was poorly run by a faction-ridden communist party. The new government announced ill-conceived, broad-sweeping reforms that alienated large sections of the populace, yet it did little to implement the reforms – alienating the remaining section of the populace that might have supported them. In 1979, Prime Minister Amin assassinated President Taraki. Taraki was Moscow's man and Amin was not. Amin continued to request Soviet aid, including military intervention to help fight the growing Mujahideen threat.

However, Amin did not accept orders from Moscow as readily as his predecessor. The DRA was spinning out of control and Moscow intended to do something about it. They decided to eliminate Amin and put their own candidate in power while using a seemingly reluctant intervention to aid the DRA fight against the Mujahideen as cover. It was a successful cover. The DRA General Staff cooperated with the Soviet General Staff in planning the entry of the initial three-division Soviet force. It was a brilliant operation. At the cost of 66 Soviet dead (44 due to accidents), the Soviets controlled the cities and government of Afghanistan. Their plan was to hold the cities, garrisons and airfields while the armed forces of the DRA combated the Mujahideen in the countryside. They anticipated that they would be there for two or three years. Little did they imagine that they were now involved in the middle of a civil war on extremely rugged terrain where the Soviets, not the DRA, would carry the bulk of the combat burden.

THE INITIAL INSURGENCY

The Soviets invaded in December and there was little initial resistance. However, with the spring thaw, resistance began to mount.

Initially, tribal leaders assembled large armies (*lashkars*) that marched on the Soviet garrisons. They were easy targets for Soviet artillery and air power. It became very clear to the tribal leaders that large tribal armies could not oppose the Soviets and DRA, but that guerrilla warfare offered possibilities. They turned to the Mujahideen who were already conducting guerrilla warfare.

Pre-invasion Soviet military planning estimated that they would need 30–35 divisions to conquer and control Afghanistan completely. It soon became clear that the initial three Soviet divisions were inadequate. Eventually, the Soviets fielded five and two-thirds division equivalents in Afghanistan. They needed far more however, this was the maximum amount that could be supplied over the over-burdened Afghan road network. Soviet efforts to use theater logistics from the Soviet military districts broke down at the Afghan border.

The Soviet Union had a good deal of experience with guerrilla warfare. During the 1920s and 1930s, it conducted a successful counterinsurgency in Central Asia against the *Basmachi*. During World War II, the Soviet Union fielded and directed the largest partisan force ever deployed in wartime. Following World War II, the Soviets conducted another successful counter insurgency in the Ukraine. Yet, when the Soviets entered Afghanistan, they were unprepared to conduct a counterinsurgency in this theater. Their divisions were designed for conventional war against NATO or China, so they had all their tanks, chemical defense and air defense units with them. The Soviet intention was to hold the operational key terrain and ward off the hostile neighboring states of Pakistan and Iran. The armed forces of the DRA were supposed to fight the counter-insurgency. However, as the countryside rose in revolt, it became obvious that the DRA could not handle the counterinsurgency alone and that the Soviets would have to participate – as the main partner.

The initial Mujahideen resistance to the Soviets was based on a popular uprising. Hundreds of small bands took to the field. The guerrillas were local and their leaders were local – village chiefs, tribal leaders, prominent family elders. The revolt was secular and the leadership was secular. The local mullahs and imams might accompany the guerrillas, but seldom in a leadership role. Since the guerrillas were local, the support base was built in. Food, water, shelter and medical aid were readily available and the neighbors provided intelligence on Soviet and DRA movements. The guerrillas' weapons were what they had on hand – primarily World War I-era

British Lee-Enfield .303 bolt-action rifles and older British Martini-Henry single-shot breech-loading rifles from the 1880s. Lucky units seized DRA district headquarters, looting their arms rooms and liberating AK-47 Kalashnikov assault rifles and some machine guns.

Belatedly the Soviets addressed the insurgency. Despite their past experience, they had forgotten their history. They read Mao Tse-tung's aphorism 'the guerrilla is the fish that swims in the ocean of the people'. The Soviets decided that the way to isolate the fish was to drain the ocean. The Soviet Air Force, which had readily ripped apart the Afghan *lashkars*, was useless against a guerrilla that it could not target. However, the air force could readily target irrigation systems, orchards, cropland, farms, villages and livestock. The air force went after the Mujahideen support structure.

At this time, Afghanistan was a country of approximately 17 million people. Most were rural. Soviet bombing drove 5.5 million people out of the country and into refugee camps in bordering Pakistan and Iran. Another 2.2 million became 'internal refugees' crowding into the shantytowns and the suburbs of Afghanistan's cities to escape the Soviet Air Force. The guerrilla now had to carry his weapon, ammunition, food and water with him. If he was hurt, his closest medical support might be in Pakistan or Iran. The rural social system was turned upside down and the guerrillas' support base was being closed down.

The Soviets soon learned that they did not want to be within 300 meters of the Mujahideen. The 300-meter mark represents the maximum effective range of the Kalashnikov assault rifle, the RPG-7 anti-tank grenade launcher against a moving target and is well within the danger close area of supporting artillery and air power. The Mujahideen preferred the flat trajectory fight where the bulk of Soviet combat power was negated. Where possible, the Soviets bulldozed orchards, villages and other cover and concealment some 300 meters back from both sides of the road to create stand-off and aid in counter-ambush and deployed millions of land mines to keep the Mujahideen at bay.

THE INSURGENCY MATURES

The insurgency was in trouble. The Mujahideen were unpaid volunteers who provided their own weapons and food. Their support base was being driven out of the countryside and, in places, it was difficult to get close enough to the Soviets to engage them effectively. They needed weapons with greater ranges and supplies.

Afghanistan's neighbors were uneasy about the Soviet incursion. Pakistan, bracketed by India and Afghanistan, was particularly threatened since archenemy India was a close friend of the Soviet Union. Pakistan lost Bangladesh in the 1973 war and consequently recast itself from a secular to an Islamic state as a defensive move against India. Pakistan became an Islamic Republic to gain worldwide Islamic support to offset India's overwhelming advantages in manpower and economic viability. Iran was also threatened, particularly since it was fighting a bloody war with Iraq, a good customer and friend of the Soviet Union. Pakistan and Iran began providing aid to the Mujahideen. The US, People's Republic of China, Britain, France, Italy, Saudi Arabia, Egypt and the United Arab Emirates (UAE) began funneling military and humanitarian aid to the Mujahideen through Pakistan. Pakistan's assessment was that the Soviet Union had come to Afghanistan to stay and it was in Pakistan's best interest to support those Mujahideen who would never accept the Soviet presence. The Pakistan Inter-Services Intelligence Agency (ISI) began to funnel aid through various Afghan political factions headquartered in Pakistan. Eventually there were seven major Afghan factions receiving aid. The politics of these factions were determined by their leaders' (three of which were Islamic moderates and four of which were Islamic fundamentalists) religious convictions. Pakistan required that the various ethnic and tribal Mujahideen groups join one of the factions in order to receive aid. The Pakistanis favored the most fundamentalist groups and rewarded them accordingly. This aid gave Afghan clerics accompanying the Mujahideen unprecedented power in the conduct of the war and undermined the traditional authority of the tribal and village chiefs.

The seven factions in Pakistan were:

- The Afghanistan National Liberation Front (ANLF) – *Jebh-e-Nejat-i-Melli Afghanistan* – was a moderate party founded by Sebqhatullah Mojadeddi. Primarily secular, it drew from the tribes, the old social order and the Sufi orders of the south. Its strength was in Kunar and Paktia provinces. It has Deobandi links.
- The Islamic Party (HIH) – *Hezb-e-Islamie-i-Gulbuddin* – founded in 1974 to fight the Daoud government. It later split as cofounders Rabanni and Khalis founded their own factions. Its

leader, Gulbuddin Hikmatyar, is a fundamentalist internationalist Pashtun. His radical Islamist party recruited heavily from among the government secular school and Kabul religious school graduates. Hikmatyar's party received more outside aid from Pakistan, the US and Saudi Arabia than any other party. Its strength was in Nuristan, Nangrahar and around Kabul.

- Islamic Party (HIK) – *Hezb-e-Islami-Khalis* – was founded by Mawlawi Mohammed Yunis Khalis who left Afghanistan for Pakistan in 1973 after the Daoud coup. Khalis is from Nangrahar Province and is very anti-Shia. His most famous commanders included Abdul Haq in Kabul, Haji Abdul Qadir in Nangrahar and Jalladuddin Hagani of Paktia Province. The party is fundamentalist moderate. Its recruits came from graduates of government schools, religious schools of the Gilhzai, Khugiangi and Jadran tribes as well as the Kabul and Kandahar regions. It also drew a lot of army deserters. Its strength was in Nangrahar, Kabul, Kunar, Lowgar and Wardak provinces.
- Islamic Revolutionary Movement (IRMA) – *Harakat-e-Inqilab-i-Islami* – was founded by Mohammad Nabi Mohammadi. The party is moderate (traditional Islamist) and primarily Pashtun. It drew recruits from the private seminaries, liberal intellectuals, and the Andar, Gilhzai, Mahmund, Hotak and Durrani tribes. Its strength was in Lowgar Province and the Helmand valley. General Yahyah Nawroz was one of its most famous commanders.
- Islamic Society (JIA) – *Jamiat-i-Islami* – was founded by a Tajik, Burhanud-din Rabbani, who fled to Pakistan in 1974. His most famous commanders were Ahmed Shah Masood in the Panjshir valley and Ismail Khan in Herat Province. The party is primarily moderate fundamentalist and dominated by ethnic Tajiks, but has Uzbeks and Pashtun in its ranks. Its recruits came from the religious and secular government schools and northern Sunni religious schools and northern Sufi brotherhoods. Its strength was in northern Afghanistan. It had members throughout Afghanistan but was particularly strong in Lowgar, Samangan, Faryab, Farah and Nimroz provinces.
- Islamic Union for the Liberation of Afghanistan (IUA) – *Ittihad-I-Islami* – was founded by Abd Al-Rab Abdul-Rassul Sayyaf. This used to be called the Etehad-e Islami (EIA) until 1981. The faction is militant fundamentalist and anti-Shia. In the mid-1980s, it again changed its name to the Islamic Union of Afghanistan.

The IUA was heavily financed by the Wahhabi sect out of Saudi Arabia. Sayyaf was known for recruiting motivated Arab youths for jihad in his organization.

- National Islamic Front of Afghanistan (NIFA) – *Mahaz-e-Melli* – was founded by Pir Sayed Ahmad Gailani. This moderate party attracted a number of former officers from the Afghan Army and moderate technocrats. This royalist party recruited from the landed aristocracy, the tribes and the Sufi brotherhood. The primary power base came from the Zadran, Mangal, Jaji, Ahmadzai, Tareen, Kochi and Sulemankhel tribes. The party was primarily Pashtun and its strength was in Paktia, Paktika, Ghazni and Kandahar provinces.

There were four factions headquartered in Iran. They were smaller, less well supplied, primarily Shia and their strength was in the Hazara-section of Afghanistan (the Hazarajat). They were:

- Revolutionary Council of the Islamic Union of Afghanistan-*Shura-i Inqilab-i Ittifagh-i Islami-i Afghanistan* was a traditionalist Shia party led by Sayyad Beheshti. It recruited among the Hazara peasants and social elite. Many defecting Afghan Army officers led its ranks. It had wide support in the Hazarajat and Ghazni Province.
- The Islamic Victory Organization of Afghanistan – *Sazman-i Nasr-i Islami-yi Afghanistan* – was a radical Islamist party led by a council that recruited from young Hazara who were educated in Iran. This pro-Iran party was headquartered in Daykundi.
- Islamic Movement (HI) – *Harakat-i-Islami* – was founded by Ayatollah Asef Muhsini in Iran as a Shia faction. The party has a traditional Islamic orientation. It recruited educated Shia from all ethnic groups. Its most famous commander was Mohammad Anwari who fought in the Turkmen valley, west of Kabul.
- Army of the Guardians of the Revolution – *Sepah-i Pasdaran* – is a radical Islamist party led by Akbari and Saddiqi. It had very close ties with the Iranian government. It had few fighters but drew from clerics who were disaffected with Behesti's Shura.

The Mujahideen were unpaid volunteers with family responsibilities. This meant that they were part-time warriors and the spoils of war played a major role in military actions. Usually, one-fifth of the booty taken in an ambush belonged to the ambush commander and the remainder was divided among the participants. Mujahideen sold captured weapons and equipment in the bazaars to support their families. As the war progressed, mobile Mujahideen groups emerged. The mobile Mujahideen groups were larger and consisted of young (under 25), unmarried, better-trained warriors. Sometimes the mobile Mujahideen were paid. The mobile Mujahideen ranged over a much larger area of operations than the local Mujahideen and were more responsive to the plans and desires of the factions.

The US and Britain gave their aid in the form of weapons, equipment and supplies. Saudi Arabia and the UAE gave their aid in the form of cash. Often the aid that was available was inappropriate for the individual Mujahideen commander. For example, a commander might arrive in Pakistan seeking anti-tank mines, only to discover that no anti-tank mines were available, but heavy machine gun ammunition was being distributed. The commander might have no heavy machine guns, but he would take the ammunition anyway and take it down to the bazaar and sell it. There would be a resultant hue and cry that the Mujahideen were selling aid for personal gain. Actually, what usually happened was that the commander would then take the money to buy the anti-tank mines at the bazaar, where everything always seemed to be available.

Transporting weapons, ammunition and supplies was also a challenge. Pick-up trucks, mules (in the mountains) and camels (in the desert) were optimum supply transport for the Mujahideen. As the supply convoy would move from one tribal area to another, the tribe would exact a ten per cent toll on the goods. Transport was paid for in advance. Since the US and Britain gave no cash aid which could be used for transport fees, additional supplies were sold to pay for transport. Some Mujahideen groups tried to organize their own transport units, but quickly discovered that the local teamsters were strong and aggressive enough to make this an unviable option. Local teamsters hauled for the Mujahideen. As with all teamsters, negotiations were part of the process. The commander may want his supplies delivered to point A. However, no teamster likes to 'run bobtail' and wants a return load. The teamster might want to deliver to point B instead, where he could pick up lumber, lapis lazuli, heroin or whatever the return cargo was.

Commanders were responsible for losses of transport mules, trucks and camels to Soviet actions. Soviet helicopter gunships were quick to attack pack animals and trucks. The introduction of heavy weaponry created a surge in the demand for transport, but there was a decrease, rather than an increase, in available transport.

By 1984, there were clearly not enough mules to meet the needs of the insurgency. The US responded by buying large numbers of American mules to ease the crisis. The American mules were flown over to Pakistan, but there were still problems. The American mules were much bigger than the locals and ate twice as much as the locals. They also carried less – and they began to die from the many virulent diseases endemic to Afghanistan. Attempts to import other pack animals from around the Middle East were not much more successful.

THE MATURE INSURGENCY

The Mujahideen were forced to build a series of supply depots, supply points and forward supply points inside Afghanistan to ease their logistics dilemma. They established these in remote, inaccessible areas in mountains and canyons. Tora Bora, Zhawar and the Sharikot valley are prime examples. These sites aided supply but cost the Mujahideen mobility since they were forced to defend them. These sites gave the Soviets something to target.

The Soviets were not having an easy time of it either. The Soviets found that it took some 85 per cent of their force and DRA forces to provide basic security – guarding cities, industry, airfields, garrisons and outposts along the supply routes from the Soviet Union. This left 15 per cent of the force available to go after the Mujahideen. The forces that fought the Mujahideen were primarily airborne, air assault and Spetsnaz. The two Spetsnaz brigades' primary mission was convoy and caravan interdiction.

Soviet forces were bleeding in Afghanistan, but the biggest threat was disease. Over 60 per cent of the Soviet service personnel were hospitalized for disease during their normal two-year tour of duty. Shigellosis, amoebeosis, typhus, cholera, hepatitis and other water-borne diseases plagued the force. Malaria was also a problem. However, Soviet casualties and disease were hidden from the Soviet people. The Soviet media did an effective job limiting the reporting on Afghanistan to positive events. The Soviet military also kept non-accredited foreign journalists at bay. Further, the hazardous trip inside and the lengthy process to get the story out discouraged most

Western journalists from covering the war effectively. Most preferred long-range reporting from Pakistan, relying on press releases from the factions.

Mujahideen offensive tactics included the ambush, the raid, the shelling attack, mine warfare, attacks on strong points, blocking lines of communication and conducting sieges. Mujahideen defensive tactics included defending against raids, fighting helicopter insertions, defending against a cordon and search, defending base camps, counter ambush and fighting in encirclement. They also developed a set of tactics for the urban guerrilla.

Soviet offensive tactics included the combined-arms attack, the advance to contact, the cordon and search, the air assault, the base camp siege, the base camp attack, the clearing attack, the raid, the ambush, the artillery offensive, air interdiction and encirclement. Soviet defensive tactics included mine warfare, march and convoy escort, strong-point defense, patroling and mobile defense.

By 1984, the war was primarily a logistics war with each side trying to strangle the other's logistics while striving to stay supplied and viable. The war was stalemated, but no one in the Soviet Politburo was making any decisions during the 'twilight of the General Secretaries'. Brezhnev, Chernenko, Andropov – one infirm Soviet leader after another tottered slowly to their deaths. Finally, in 1985, a comparative youngster, Mikhail Gorbachev, came to power. Shortly after his assumption of power, the Soviet military launched the bloodiest fighting of the war. The Mujahideen were badly battered and close to breaking, but the Soviets did not realize it. In 1986, Gorbachev announced 'Afghanization' of the war and the eventual withdrawal of Soviet forces from Afghanistan. Soviet combat fell off significantly.

By 15 February 1989, the last of the Soviet combat forces had withdrawn from Afghanistan. However, confident predictions that the DRA would soon collapse after the withdrawal were not realized. The DRA outlasted the Soviet Union. The faction-ridden Mujahideen had difficulty converting from a guerrilla force to a conventional force to defeat the DRA.

MUJAHIDEEN LESSONS LEARNED

1. Guerrilla warfare is a long-term proposition. Persistence and patience are required for victory. The occupier must be worn-down

and demoralized. The battle can be won politically in the homeland of the occupier. Survival is more important than tactical victory.

2. The impact of high-technology weapons, such as jet aircraft and helicopters, can be negated by camouflage, heat shields, decoys and dispersion. However, these systems can have a major impact on the local populace.

3. The support or neutrality of the local populace is essential for logistics support, intelligence and survival. Local guerrillas have a natural advantage. Non-local guerrillas gain or maintain support by frequently passing units through disputed areas, conducting shelling attacks and mining incidents to depict strength and activity.

4. Sanctuary is essential. Safe areas in Pakistan and Iran were vital to guerrilla bands for supply, medical treatment, resting, training and refitting. The Soviets carefully observed the international borders, although the locals and guerrillas did not.

5. Logistics support is essential, particularly as the insurgency grows and acquires heavy weapons. Logistics support may involve establishing depots and supply points inside the country and then defending them. Cash is often preferred to actual supplies. If aid is given in supplies, cash should also be provided for transport.

6. Close combat is the preferred option. It is best to get close to the enemy for the flat-trajectory fight where the enemy cannot use his artillery, mortars and aircraft.

7. When deploying heavy weapons, firing sites must be carefully prepared so that the weapons can be quickly moved out of the area or into a bunker or cave. Ambushes, raids and shelling attacks must be rapidly executed and the sites rapidly evacuated to avoid retaliation.

8. Communications are hard to maintain and readily intercepted. Messengers, visual signals and meetings are more secure than radio.

9. Publicity and media support is essential but tough to attain. Western journalists do not always want to travel to where the fighting is.

10. Adjustments in tactics are necessary only when enemy technology dictates that change. The anti-personnel land mine and the helicopter gunship were new technology that threatened traditional war-fighting and forced changes in guerrilla tactics.

THE INSURGENCY

There was both a religious-based and a secular insurgency. The religious-based insurgency began in the early 1970s on the campus of Kabul University. The Islamic Youth movement found several adherents, including Gulbuddin Hekmatyar and Burhanuddin Rabbani. After brushes with the law, they fled to the countryside and then on to Pakistan to oppose the king. When the king was overthrown, other dissidents joined their cause to fight the new president. However, the religious-based insurgency was a relatively small movement.

When the president was overthrown by a communist coup, the insurgency grew with the addition of guerrillas opposing the atheism of the new movement. However, the main opposition was secular. It was a rural rebellion opposed to the communist reforms in land ownership, women's rights and rural landlord-renter relations. When the Soviets intervened, the insurgency grew dramatically. Initially, however, it was a secular-led rebellion with the primary goal to expel the Soviets. The fact that the Soviet Union was an atheist state aided the cause. The insurgency became more of a religious struggle as the religious-based aid distribution scheme began to distribute significant amounts of military weapons and supplies.

There was no common vision of the type of government that a successful insurgency would create. Some factions wanted to restore the monarchy. Others wanted to create a secular republic. Others wanted to create a moderate Islamist state governed by Sharia law. Still others wanted to create an Islamic Emirate governed by strict Sharia law. Some of the most radical saw Afghanistan as the center of a radical Islamist movement that would spread across the region and beyond.

The professional military officers who quit the armed forces of Afghanistan were generally kept from key leadership roles in the insurgency. The fundamentalist religious leaders saw them as threats to their positions and as being too secular. The secular leaders saw them as threats to their positions. Some military personnel led guerrilla bands, but many more served as staff officers – planning actions, coordinating logistics, conducting training and providing intelligence analysis.

The insurgency enjoyed popular support throughout the country, but was centered in the rural villages. The more liberal city dwellers were more tolerant of reform and change, but many still resented the presence of Soviet armed forces. Small urban guerrilla cells formed in the cities, but their freedom of movement, and prospects of survival, were limited. Throughout the insurgency, the guerrillas tried to capture and hold a city in which to proclaim a provisional government, but they never succeeded (Orgun was the city that the Mujahideen tried to capture most often).

The Mujahideen were joined by foreigners from around the Islamic world. They brought money and international support with them. Their presence caused a deal of friction with some factions, since the foreigners were considered prima donnas who were there for jihad-credit. They were considered ill-disciplined, unwilling to share the burdens of campaigning and had a reputation for executing DRA prisoners in front of video cameras. DRA prisoners were usually conscripts and the Mujahideen usually offered them a chance to switch sides and paroled them home if they did not.

Material support of the insurgency came from a variety of states with a variety of motives:

a. The US, smarting from the support that the Soviet Union had provided North Vietnam and the Vietcong during the Vietnam War, looked on aid as a way of reciprocating and giving the Soviet Union 'a bloody nose'. NATO allies Britain, France, Italy and West Germany provided varying aid in support of the US effort.

b. China and the Soviet Union were competing for control of the world communist movement and inroads into the Third World. China and the Soviet Union had recently fought each other in border skirmishes along the Ussuri River in the Far East. China aided the insurgency to support its contest with the Soviet Union.

c. Saudi Arabia, Egypt and the UAE supported the insurgency as a Sunni reaction to an atheist invasion of another Sunni state. Clergy within those states, particularly those of the Wahabbi sect, provided private funding and proselytizing, to the insurgency.

d. Pakistan and Iran helped the insurgents since they felt their own borders were threatened by the Soviet Union. They were also maneuvering politically in order to strengthen their claims to disputed territory with Afghanistan.

e. Islamic clergy in many lands conducted fundraising in support of the insurgency. The Deobandi and Wahabbi sects provided funding as did Sufi and Shia communities.

f. The refugees in the Iranian and Pakistani camps provided aid –
    not so much financially as morally. Mujahideen families were
    usually in the camps. The camps were also fertile recruiting
    grounds for new Mujahideen.

THE GOVERNMENT OF THE DEMOCRATIC REPUBLIC OF AFGHANISTAN

The DRA had most of its support in the cities. Although it tried
to follow the Marxist-Leninist model for establishing socialism/
communism throughout the countryside, its power in the countryside was limited to army garrisons, province capitals and district
capitals, key economic facilities and main roads. Many of the district
capitals were not under DRA control. Several district 'governments'
might be crowded into one capital since the DRA officials could not
govern, let alone survive, in their appointed place of duty.

The DRA tried a variety of programs, included armed propaganda teams, to win the populace over. The armed propaganda
teams provided free food, medical treatment and plays to villagers
as they traveled from village trying to drum up support.

The DRA, realizing that their atheist trappings were costing
support, tried to incorporate Islam into the government. They created
a Ministry of Religious Affairs to try to patch over differences and
support friendly clergy. To garner the support of non-party members,
non-communist officials were designated throughout the government. However, the DRA government faithfully copied the Soviet
model. The KHAD was a copy of the KGB – a strong, uniformed
service that maintained a separate armed force. The Sarandoy mim-
icked the Soviet Ministry of Internal Affairs (MVD) as an armed
police force with military capability. Young Afghan communists
copied the Soviet Komsomol members in trying to rally support to
the government while spearheading movements in the countryside.
DRA armed propaganda teams visited rural villages to put on plays,
provide medical aid and attempt to rally support. The DRA also
raised, armed and funded local militias to protect their villages from
the Mujahideen.

The KHAD (later the WAD) provided the most accurate human
intelligence (HUMINT) on Mujahideen forces. The KHAD ran
agent nets and paid informers to provide intelligence for DRA and
Soviet forces to act on. The most serious defect of the KHAD net

was that agents were frequently days away from their handler and by the time they had hiked out with the information, the information was dated and often useless. Still, the KHAD provided the best HUMINT available to the DRA and Soviet forces. The KHAD also emulated the KGB in interrogation techniques and infiltration of the DRA Armed Forces. It was the regime's insurance that it would not be replaced in the same fashion that it had replaced the Daoud government.

The Sarandoy served as a national police force, but their armaments surpassed the traditional police arms of pistol, baton and shotgun. The Sarandoy constituted a third ground force within the DRA. They had heavy armaments, armored personnel carriers and a separate command and control system. The DRA Army, KHAD and Sarandoy often worked together out of necessity, but they were separate, rival systems designed to counterbalance one another and prevent regime ouster. It was not an efficient, or particularly effective design, but the DRA was designed for regime survival, not efficiency or effectiveness. Furthermore, the DRA leadership saw their chief threat as internal subversion within the communist party instead of the rural Mujahideen.

The DRA Armed Forces were also based on the Soviet Armed Forces, and their organization, equipment, training and command and control were Soviet-furnished or inspired. Soviet military advisers served down to the separate battalion level. DRA air defense units, chemical units, armored and mechanized units emphasized that this army was organized for conventional combat, not counterinsurgency. Many, if not most, of the professional officer corps from the royal and Daoud regimes had left to join the resistance or had been purged by the communists. Many of the officers educated in the Soviet Union also left or were purged. Desertion, poor leadership and poor morale plagued this conscript-based army. DRA outposts were surrounded by dense anti-personnel minefields – emplaced as much to keeping the conscripts from deserting as to keeping the Mujahideen out. Loyalty within the DRA Army was suspect and riddled with Mujahideen sympathizers and informants. The Soviet military was reluctant to share operational data and planning with the DRA, since the information was often leaked to the Mujahideen. There were some excellent Afghan Army units. The 38th Commando Brigade was a premier force until it was destroyed on hot landing zones during the opening of the Second Battle of Zhawar. The 15th Tank Brigade was a first-rate unit that became the regime's ready reaction force, moving from point to point where the demand was the greatest and armor could operate.

The government and economic structure of the DRA were also poor copies of the Soviet Union. Soviet political, bureaucratic and economic advisers worked with their Afghan counterparts attempting to create another 'socialist workers paradise' in Afghanistan. Although token non-communists occupied some 'show place' positions within the government, the communist party was clearly in control. During the war, the DRA even allowed some non-communist political parties, but they were controlled and directed by the communists.

THE SOVIET 40TH ARMY

The Soviet 40th Army was originally composed of the 5th Motorized Rifle Division and the 180th Motorized Rifle Division (both mobilization divisions) and the 103rd Guards Airborne Division. The first two divisions, drawn from the Central Asian Military District, contained a high number of Uzbeks, Turkmens, Tajiks and Kyrghiz – traditionally Islamic peoples. Shortly afterwards, the 201st Motorized Rifle Division entered the country. It was also drawn from the Central Asian Military District. Only the airborne division was a ready division. The others drew on reservists from the region – mostly Central Asians with some form of Islamic tradition in the family past. Most of these reservists were withdrawn within 12 months of their commitment and replaced by new conscripts drawn from across the Soviet Union. Much has been made of this replacement in the West. The inference drawn was that the Central Asians proved unreliable, sympathetic to their Islamic brothers or even a fifth column for the propagation of fundamentalist Islam within the Soviet Union. While there may be some elements of truth in these allegations, the simple fact is that they were reservists and their reserve time was up. The Supreme Soviet would have had to pass a law extending their time and it was not worth it.

The Soviet 40th Army was outfitted for war on rolling plains with NATO or China. The 40th Army brought its full complement of tanks, air defense artillery, chemical protection units and all the other paraphernalia for conventional war against a modern mechanized force. Soon, the Soviets began sending home tank and air defense regiments and brigades and replacing them with more infantry.

Tactics, troop formations and equipment were modified or replaced to meet the onerous conditions of Afghanistan. More helicopters and SU-25 close air support aircraft were brought into the fight. The Soviet Army was an artillery army with a lot of tanks. Unfortunately for the Soviets, neither the tank nor the artillery piece was to dominate the fight. The Soviets needed lots of light infantry and engineers – which they never had enough of. Soviet war-fighting was built around operational success. The Soviets developed and perfected the operational art during World War II and intended to defeat NATO and China on the operational level. Operational flexibility demands a deal of tactical predictability and rigidity. Battle drills were the basis of Soviet squad and platoon tactics. Afghanistan could not be fought on the operational level. It was a tactical fight that demanded tactical flexibility. The Soviets had to reinvent tactics in the middle of a conflict.

It was also a secret war. During the first two years of the conflict, the Soviet press covered the deaths of some two dozen servicemen – though thousands had already died. Whenever Afghanistan was mentioned in the Soviet press, it showed happy Soviet servicemen building orphanages – while neglecting to mention their role in filling them. The Soviet public was kept in the dark. When a dead Soviet soldier was returned to his family, the family was sworn to secrecy in order to get the body back for burial. Even the earlier tombstones did not list where the serviceman had died, only that he had died 'fulfilling his internationalist duty'.

Afghanistan was not a sought-after assignment. Parents paid hefty bribes to keep their sons away from the conflict. After initial training, conscripts spent the rest of their two-year obligation in the war. Unlike the US experience in Vietnam, the entire officer corps did not go to Afghanistan. Less than ten per cent of the motorized rifle officers served there, but over 60 per cent of the airborne, air assault and Spetsnaz officers served. Interestingly, the tactics of the airborne, air assault and Spetsnaz changed after the war – while the armor and motorized rifle tactics did not.

SOVIET LESSONS LEARNED FROM THE WAR

1. Guerrilla war is a contest of endurance and national will. The side with the highest moral commitment will hold the ground at the end of the conflict. Battlefield victory is almost irrelevant.

2. Air domination is irrelevant unless precisely targeted.
3. Secure logistics and lines of communication are essential.
4. Conventional tactics, equipment and weapons require major adjustment or replacement.
5. Conventional war force structure is inappropriate.
6. Tanks are of limited value except as mobile reserves and a security element in cities. Light infantry and engineers are at a premium.
7. Medical support is paramount.
8. Logistics determines the scope of activity and force size either side can field.
9. The information battle is essential to maintaining external and internal support.

THE MUJAHIDEEN BACKERS

Sanctuary, training and logistics support were essential to the viability of the Mujahideen movement. Sanctuary was provided by Pakistan and Iran. Despite the uncertain borders and the refusal of all Afghan governments to recognize the Durrand line, the Soviets conscientiously kept their regular forces from violating the frontier and their air forces from over-flying the border. Naturally, the Mujahideen concentrated supplies and forces just over the border. The Pakistani ISI, the US and Britain provided training. The US, Britain, France, Italy, West Germany, China, Saudi Arabia, Egypt and the UAE provided logistics support. One of the more controversial systems provided to the Mujahideen was the US Stinger shoulder-fired air defense missile. This deadly, man-portable missile did not knock down anywhere near the number of Soviet aircraft that the Mujahideen and US backers claimed. However, this does not mean that the Stinger was ineffective. The Soviets completely revamped their aerial tactics to avoid losses to Stinger. High-performance jet aircraft flew at 15,000 feet where they were safe from the Stinger, but also ineffective. Helicopter gunships no longer ranged over the countryside, but flew in the relatively safe air space above Soviet ground forces. Transport and passenger aircraft kicked out strings of decoy flares during take off and landing.

Despite the aid, the Mujahideen backers often had difficulty controlling or directing the actions of the resistance. The independent nature of the Afghans meant that outsiders were not calling the shots. The Mujahideen would cooperate with their backers when it was to their advantage or when the backer withheld aid to force compliance. For example, the Soviets ran tactical pipelines from the Soviet Union down the eastern and western corridors of Afghanistan. They pumped diesel and aviation fuel through these pipelines. The pipelines were an easy target and lost fuel had an immediate effect on the Soviet effort. The Mujahideen had no desire to attack pipelines since there was no glory in it. Their warrior mythos overrode military common sense. The Mujahideen backers bribed, cajoled or withheld aid in order to get the pipelines attacked.

The backers had even less success in hammering together a workable coalition of Mujahideen to work together over an extended period of time. The Mujahideen were tactical fighters and extended operations had little appeal. The military officers in the Mujahideen ranks were occasionally successful in mounting and sustaining an operation, but this was rare and limited to the static defense.

Most Mujahideen backers had promised some form of post-conflict aid once the DRA was deposed. Most analysts expected the DRA to collapse within months of the Soviet withdrawal. The DRA outlived the Soviet Union. The Mujahideen guerrillas were never united in their efforts and were unable to unite to destroy the DRA. Many Mujahideen went home. Their fight was with the Soviet invader and they had no interest in who was in control in Kabul. Often guerrillas returned home to join the DRA militia. The guerrillas were unable to change into a conventional military force. Independence, individualism and factionalism plagued these efforts. Gradually, the Mujahideen backers lost interest and turned to other pursuits. When the DRA finally fell and the Mujahideen crowded into Kabul, the backers were elsewhere and the aid never came.

Afghanistan lost over 1.3 million people, the bulk of them civilians, in pursuit of this war. The Mujahideen did not defeat a superpower, but they fought it to a standstill, then stayed in the fight until the Soviets tired and went home. The economy was shattered, the population was scattered in neighboring refugee camps and across the globe. The best and brightest were living in California, Virginia, Germany, Russia, France and Dubai. The society was shattered. It was no longer a liberal Islamic country under secular rule. Tribal law and mores no longer controlled the rural youth. Now Afghanistan had a fundamentalist Islamic orientation and was rife with schism and lawlessness. The Mujahideen was no longer an unpaid volunteer. Now, he was the man with the gun who could take what he desired. Anarchy rocked the nation and threatened its neighbors. Pre-war Afghanistan may have had a ten per cent literacy rate. Few children were properly educated during the war and fewer doctors, engineers, teachers and scientists were produced. Farming was at a standstill due to the loss of irrigation systems, orchards and vineyards. Mines and unexploded ordnance cluttered the fields. Warlords battled warlords as Afghanistan took the position as the one of the poorest countries on the planet – the country that led the world in infant mortality and death in childbirth. The Mujahideen could claim victory, but it was a hollow victory indeed – a victory that eventually spawned the Taliban movement and the bloodiest ethnic civil war in Afghanistan's history.

'The War in Iraq': An Assessment of Lessons Learned by Russian Military Specialists Through 31 July 2003

TIMOTHY L. THOMAS

A host of prominent military and civilian specialists critiqued the US led coalition war against Iraq. Their comments reflected a mixture of Cold War thinking on the one hand and a new place to update the Russian armed forces on the other. Those in the latter group demanded that Russian military reform linger no longer, and that lessons learned from what transpired in Iraq be incorporated into Russian threat assessments.

Russian military experts offered varying assessments of the recent US-British led war in Iraq. For most retired members of the military establishment and for several serving officers, the coalition's techniques represented nothing new and were highly criticized. Derogatory comments were aimed at the coalition's imprecise use of precision weapons, the inability of the coalition to successfully engage the Iraqi military, and the inaccuracy of coalition reporting. In short, these Soviet or Russian officers did not believe coalition 'propaganda' about the low number of casualties or equipment failures (all the while swallowing Arab propaganda without comment), and preferred to highlight coalition failures and Iraqi successes. For the majority of serving officers, however, and a few retired officers and a civilian member of the Duma defense committee, the coalition's performance was enviable and worthy of admiration.

The difference in commentary was significant, coming as it did at a time of intense debate over military reform in Russia. The debate centered on the ability of the Russian armed forces to switch from a draft to a mixed draft and volunteer force, and to produce a modern, high-tech force capable of defending the country in the coming years. The implication of the debate was that, from the viewpoint of the retired officers and a few serving officers, not much was needed in the way of military reform. For example, former Defense Minister Igor Rodionov noted that even though the state of the armed forces is worse than critical, any attempt to create a small professional army in Russia is doomed to fail, as the economy is not ready for it.[1] From the viewpoint of a few Duma defense officials and other officers, on the other hand, military reform is not only required but long overdue.

By late July, the ongoing analysis of the war did appear to have nudged the debate over military reform in a positive direction. President Putin noted at the end of July that debate over reform is over, and that three things are required: the technical re-outfitting of the armed force, increasing the capabilities of permanent readiness units and reinforcing the officer and sergeant corps. Russia's strong human and technical potential would ensure the success of military reform, he added.[2] One wonders of course if, for the umpteenth time, this means that the old guard has won and that military reform will only be a slogan and not seriously implemented. If so, it will not bode well for the future of Russia's military, beset as it is with a long list of problems. Not only are the armed forces mired down in Chechnya against a handful of bandits, they also are constantly fighting: (a) corruption among members of the officer corps; (b) a lack of discipline in the force and a lack of reliable equipment; and (c) a military budget that is less than adequate for the task at hand. Russian military leaders, both past and present, cannot afford to continue along the same path any longer. They are gradually leading the Russian armed forces to ruin. If the armed forces stop progressing then the country's security will eventually pay for this oversight.

That is not to say that there weren't 'lessons learned' from the war in Iraq. In short, lessons were learned from the geopolitical to the tactical albeit not the ones Western experts might have expected. Some of the lessons will stand the scrutiny of time, while others will be discarded immediately. Not unexpectedly, those articulated by former Soviet officers and conservative serving officers differ in both tone and content from those offered by younger Russian officers and civilians now occupying positions from policymakers to journalists. The analysis below is limited to the written opinions of military personnel, civilian members of the Duma Defense Committee and to the commander in chief of Russia's armed forces, President Vladimir Putin. It does not include the writings of journalists, the group known as the Ramzaj group or the group of journalists and former Department of Military Intelligence (GRU) officers under the web site www.iraqwar.ru.

PROMINENT MILITARY AND CIVILIAN WRITERS

The Russian government, along with other powers, initially opposed US military intervention in Iraq, joining a group against action without a UN Security Council resolution. Russian representatives counseled delay in the start of military operations to give the inspectors more time, and Russian public opinion at the time contained strong anti-US and anti-coalition protests. Military and political elites with ties to the regime used the conflict to once again call for an anti-US stance in Russian foreign policy. After initially condemning the use of force, the Putin administration indicated that a defeat of the US was not in the interest of Russia. This pronouncement came only after several coalition successes.

Not surprisingly, former Soviet officers offered the most vehement comments against coalition actions. However, several Soviet-era officers also offered highly constructive analyses that were as good as many that current officers wrote. On the whole, civilian journalists and Russian-era officers did better in their analyses and predictions of the war's conduct and outcome. Now that the conflict has ended, all military professionals in Russia are offering more measured and insightful assessments. These domestic and military shifts provide the context for the evolution of Russian comments on lessons learned over the course of the conflict. However, one is struck by the array of differing opinions – some Soviet-era officers supported the intervention, and some Russian-era officers opposed it.

A variety of Russian journals were quick to report on the initial impressions of the war, offering the opinions of current and retired officers as well as serving members of the Duma Defense Committee. For example, in addition to the many newspapers reporting on the war, *Zarubeznoe Voennie Obozrenie (ZBO)*, or *Foreign Military Review*, reported in issue 4 of 2003 on 'Several Peculiarities of the War in Iraq', and issue 5 contained an article on 'A Chronology of Military Activity by the US Navy in Iraq'. The May/June issue of

Military Parade contained an article on the confrontation of different types of weaponry in Iraq. Issue 4 of *Morskoi Sbornik (Navy Journal)*, and the journals *Armeyski Sbornik (Army Journal)* and *Voennoyoe Mysl' (Military Thought)* also started publishing articles on lessons learned in their June and July issues. In addition to articles, several conferences were quickly organized, perhaps the most thorough and professional being an expanded session of the Russian Academy of Military Sciences Scientific Council, which was reported in the press on 28 June.

Among the prominent number of military writers or members of the Duma Defense Committee who discussed lessons learned in Iraq were the following: retired Major-General Leonid Shershnev, former deputy chief of the USSR Ministry of Defense Special Propaganda Directorate (PSYOP); retired General Major Vladimir Slipchenko, author of several prominent books on future war; former Minister of Defense, retired Marshall of the Soviet Union Dmitri Yazov; retired Major-General Vladimir Dvorkin, doctor of Technical Sciences and former chief of Russian nuclear weapons planning; General of the Army Makhmut Gareyev, president of the Academy of Military Science and long-time advisor to the Ministry of Defense; Andrei Kokoshin, former Assistant Minister of Defense and head of Russia's National Security Council, now serving as a member of the Duma; retired Major-General Aleksandr Vladimirov, vice-president of the College of Military Experts; retired Colonel-General Leonid Ivashov, former head of the Main Directorate of International Military Cooperation; Aleksey Arbatov, current Deputy Chairman of the Duma Defense Committee; and General of the Army Andrey Nikolayev, former chief of the Russian Border Guards and currently Chairman of the State Duma Defense Committee.

There were many other military writers on the subject of the coalition intervention into Iraq and the actions outcome, and some are included in the analysis below. The collection of lessons learned for this article ended on 31 July. Other lessons, more detailed and thoughtful, probably will appear later as more data is accumulated.

In some cases, as with some US and foreign analysts, Soviet/ Russian assessments turned out to be totally wrong. Some errors occurred due to the pace of operations and the failure of the Iraqi people to fight while others were caused due to either a Soviet-era mindset or a clear reliance on past experiences and trends.

RETIRED SOVIET AND RUSSIAN-ERA OFFICERS

Retired Major General Leonid Shershnev, a former psychological operations officer, apparently misunderstood or underestimated coalition PSYOP Operations. Shershnev noted on Russian television that two coalition myths – that it would win the war and that it was acting in accordance with UN sanctions – both failed. In fact, he added, the coalition conducted anti-propaganda against itself. Shershnev felt that scary leaflets worked against the Americans, and he viewed the coalition effort as primitive and shocking. He believed this demonstrated that the US had developed no new ideas.[3]

Shershnev followed up his television appearance with an article that discussed the same issues. He added that for the first time, the coalition PSYOP failures represented an information warfare defeat for the West. Most importantly, Shershnev stated Russia must 'add the information component into military art' since whoever wins the electronic mass media wins the war.[4] How information is managed and by whom is important. The mistake of the Americans, Shershnev concluded, is that no account was taken of the ideological and moral-psychological situation in that country. It was as if the Bush administration did not study Islamic psychology.[5]

Any US PSYOP officer would refute Shershnev's analysis. They would note that leaflets instructed Iraqi soldiers and civilians what to do and what not to do. This is a different leaflet theme from that which Shershnev expected, it appears. Leaflets informed combatants to go home instead of fight. As coalition forces came upon deserted vehicle after deserted vehicle, it should have been apparent that PSYOP was working! He also did not comprehend how much effort went into studying Islamic psychology before a simple leaflet was prepared. Pre-testing was conducted to ensure that cultural attitudes were taken into account, and so was post-testing of the effect of certain leaflets.

On 17 April 2003, a discussion of Russian expert shortcomings was printed in the Russian newspaper *Novaya Gazeta*. It offered a sharp slap in the face to some of the more prominent Soviet and Russian officers who commented on the war. Author Ilya Kriger noted that:

The trouble is not that the experts misinformed their leadership, just as they did all the rest of the public. Rather, it is that these predictions are unique from the standpoint of psychiatry. In drawing a picture of defeat of the American army for themselves and for us, domestic prognosticators were first and foremost consoling themselves and us with the latent idea everything is fine in the Russian Army. That we do not need a professional army. That we can make do without equipment and new weapons.[6]

The most prominent Soviet commentator with such a negative view of the US, in Kriger's view, was former Marshall of the USSR and Minister of Defense Dmitriy Yazov, who stated that:

The Iraqis are very reminiscent of us at Stalingrad . . . The moral-psychological, and that means also the combat qualities, of the allied soldiers are dubious. They are much too soft . . . and look at how they are adorned with all kinds of junk! . . When we went on the attack . . . we threw away our backpacks and our gas masks – everything except our weapons. And we did not do too badly. But here, half-naked Iraqis, fighting lightly clad, are generally tormenting the wonderfully equipped mercenaries.[7]

Yazov most likely would offer an entirely different opinion if he were interviewed today. High-technology equipment and a force trained in that equipment enabled a quick defeat of the Iraqi armed forces. Further, coalition soldiers did not turn out to be as soft as Yazov expected.

Retired Major General Vladimir Slipchenko is one Soviet-era officer who also served in the era of the Russian army. His analysis did not fit the mold of Shershnev and Yazov. He has made a new career out of staying current in his thinking and writing, and has emerged as a highly respected author of contemporary affairs. However, Slipchenko also made mistakes with his predictions of how the war would be conducted. He attempted on several occasions to interject corrections during the course of the war, but only a few of these turned out to be correct.

Before the war, General Slipchenko, author of several works on non-contact (which means stand-off war using precision weapons) and future war, offered several predictions about the emerging conflict. These predictions had worked for the conflicts in Kosovo and Afghanistan. He stated that:

- There will be no ground operations in Iraq.
- The US will enter a burning desert, as the Iraqis will certainly set fire to the oilfields.
- Some 400–500 sea- and air-based precision cruise missiles will be launched every 24 hours.
- At least 500,000 people will be killed.

- There will not be a meeting engagement on the battlefield. The US will wage a non-contact war, using precision missile strikes to destroy all key facilities in Iraq
- New pulse bombs will be used.
- Several new types of precision cruise missiles will be tested, first and foremost attention will be directed to missile launches from submarines.
- The world oil price will fall to $12–$15 a barrel.[8]

Slipchenko's analysis might have been off the mark, but it was understandable how he arrived at these calculations. He expected a replay of the Mother of All Battles (as substantiated by US actions in Kosovo some eight years later) this time on Iraqi soil and with an additional ten years of new weaponry. But the battle did not occur as Slipchenko or most analysts expected. This means that attempting to template US campaigns and operations is a risky business. The US is adept at seeking out critical vulnerabilities and peculiarities of an enemy force that are then included in the planning and conduct of such complex operations. Much depends on the situation at hand, and how to go about it in the most efficient way.

Slipchenko was taken to task for his analysis by some prominent Soviet-era authors such as Vasiliy Reznichenko whose works on Soviet tactics and operational art are well known to students of Soviet military art. He believes that a serious study of the phenomenon of war in the modern era still has not been undertaken, and therefore experts such as Slipchenko make mistakes. Reznichenko criticized Slipchenko in particular for trying to introduce US-inspired military reform into the organizational development of Russia's armed forces, and for Slipchenko's statement that by 2010–20 ground forces would become useless. However, Reznichenko did not offer his own view of future war, noting only that Russia must use computer analyses and practical exercises in place of theoretical arguments to make decisions on future force structure. He also warned that politicians must be more involved in analyzing and providing conclusions about military activities of nations worldwide.[9]

In April, Slipchenko wrote that US centralized command and control of the operation had failed and the aims of the military campaign had changed. The overall objective of overthrowing Hussein had been replaced by interim moves, such as taking a specific city, bombing a Saddam bunker, and so on. This indicated to

Slipchenko that leadership had been farmed out to commanding officers at a level lower than the Pentagon. Slipchenko also noted that a number of flying accidents were caused by a lack of training for young pilots. Here again it appears Slipchenko is using his Soviet prism and assuming that US pilots receive little training. This was not the case, as accidents were caused more often than not by something as simple as not turning on the identification signal (friend or foe) of the jet fighter. Air operations remained as complicated as during the Gulf War, and US pilots were more than up to the task of fulfilling their missions. Slipchenko did predict that Shahids or fedayeen would become a serious problem for allied troops, since they would conduct suicide bomber raids and die to fulfill their sacred duty.[10]

At the end of April, Slipchenko tried to explain his inaccurate predictions, but came up short. He wrote that Iraq had succeeded in drawing the coalition into contact warfare. This was actually the coalition's decision, not Iraq's, since ground forces were sent into Iraq immediately. He did correctly predict that the US would not use nuclear weapons, a counterpoint he made to a proclamation by a prominent Soviet-era author who predicted the use of nuclear weapons in the Gulf by the coalition.[11]

After the war had ended, Major General Aleksandr Vladimirov, vice-president of the Collegium of Military Experts, assessed the lessons and threats for Russia from the war in Iraq. Vladimirov was an assistant to the Minister of Defense of the USSR for military reform, and an advisor to the Russian Federation Supreme Soviet. His service, like Slipchenko's, spans both Soviet and Russian times.

Vladimirov noted in a 2 May interview that the war in Iraq ended due to a new strategic paradigm: contract war. By this he meant that the Iraqi leaders were somehow paid off to end the fighting.[12] In a 15 June interview he wrote:

The road to victory was liberally paved with dollars and it was namely that, and not the high-precision weaponry, that brought the Americans success. Note how bravely and stubbornly the defenders of Basra held out. Why? Because they were cut off from the commanders in Baghdad, and did not receive any orders except the initial ones. On the other hand, a major National Guard force in Karbala, a hundred kilometers south of the capital, which could have struck at the rear and flank of the American forces during the dust storm, sat inactive. That is why the military of Iraq did not blow up any bridges or dams.[13]

Vladimirov had other interesting observations as well. He noted that willpower is the main factor in war today, and that the dictatorial regime in Iraq had sapped the Iraqi Arab passion to resist. He also noted that 'Russia is still not ready to concern itself with the problem of dividing up America's legacy' (a reference to an earlier opinion of Vladimirov's that the US will start to fall apart in the next 50 years) and must prevent its own armed forces from falling apart 'by military district'. Finally he stated that Russia needs an army with a new genetic code, one based on an ideology of state, real professionalism and internal ethics. Simultaneously, Vladimirov noted that the Americans do not understand what a professional army is all about, adding 'they consider their own army to be volunteer'.[14] Perhaps he was implying that the US armed forces are a contract force, not a volunteer force. The reader was left with the impression that Vladimirov was confused about the difference in a professional, volunteer, contract and mercenary armed force.

Another analyst of the war whose service spanned both the Soviet and Russian eras is General Vladimir Dvorkin. His analysis focused on four lessons, and offered a most interesting assessment of what the coalition victory meant for Russia's forces, an assessment more realistic than those offered above.

First, he stated that the Russian armed forces needed multi-option planning, along with appropriate computer systems. Professionals must be able, in time of trouble, to react to unpredictable developments and correct current plans.

Second, Russia must urgently try to reduce the technological gap between its armed forces and those in the West. Dvorkin noted that Russia is not years but a whole epoch behind some nations. This will require enormous changes in Russia's military-industrial policy.

The third lesson was that 'it is now necessary not so much to preserve as to reproduce professional cadres' for the Russian armed forces. There is no cadre corps of junior officers, and the proportion of people eligible for the draft has fallen to almost one-tenth of the total draft resource. Dvorkin noted that the present-day Russian draftee would hardly be able to use the personal gear of coalition soldiers in Iraq, crammed as they are with communications and life-support equipment.

Fourth, and most caustically, Dvorkin added that more than ten years of reform time have been ineptly lost, and it is impermissible to continue with today's limp imitation of military reform. These reforms and new equipment are not needed to fight the West as they might have been in the past, in Dvorkin's view, but rather to partici-pate in coalition groupings on equal terms when countering challenges and threats.[15] Dvorkin's comments appear to be highly appropriate and one of the clearer analyses of the conflict for the future of Russia.

On 7 May, together with Yury Fyodorov, Deputy Director of the Institute for Applied International Research, Dvorkin wrote a follow-up article. Dvorkin and Fyodorov wrote that a key objective of military reform is to try to bridge the technological gap or to halt its menacing growth. Priority should be placed on precision weaponry integrated with intelligence, control and communication systems, and on creating joint commands. Particular attention also needs to be directed to contingency planning that combines military-strategic, operational and tactical thinking with decision-making support from special complexes of automated information-gathering devices and command and control networks.[16] He and Fyodorov noted that coalition forces had only half as much equipment and men as in the first war, and that many Russian military analysts thus concluded that a quick operation was not possible. This did not turn out to be the case as the technology of the coalition made up for the shortage in numbers.

Finally, Colonel-General Leonid Ivashov, also an officer who served during both the Soviet and Russian eras, wrote on the war's course and outcome. Ivashov was formerly the head of the Main Directorate of International Military Cooperation and was a strong critic of coalition actions in Iraq. He postulated that the coalition would use nuclear weapons in Iraq to maintain control. He offered the following conclusions about armaments in an article in *Military Parade*.

First, traditional weapons systems will remain an element of combat operations, but require upgrades to enhance their defensive effectiveness.

Second, efforts must be focused on developing electronic warfare systems that can 'strangle' links such as satellite to ground objects, aircraft carrier to combat aircraft links, and combat units to armament control systems.

Third, the entire weapon system of Russia has to be rearranged in regard to its defensive task prioritization. Decisions must be made between developing multipurpose combat aircraft and lighter and cheaper aircraft designed to counter enemy attack aircraft. In a comment unrelated to 'lessons learned' Ivashov added that the battle for Baghdad can be qualified as a loss of troop control and the inability to organize a defense. The Iraqi armed force transformed into a chaotic and confused group with isolated units that apparently became demoralized as a result.[17]

CONTEMPORARY SERVING OFFICERS OR CIVILIAN DEFENSE OFFICIALS

Individual serving Russian officers and civilian defense officials of some renown also offered their assessments of the fighting from April to the present. One such author does not meet the criteria of a serving officer or a member of the Duma Defense Committee, but still must be included based on his influence and former jobs. This person is Andrei Kokoshin, former Deputy Minister of Defense for several Defense Ministers in the 1990s and former head of the Russian Security Council, and now a State Duma Deputy. Writing in April 2003, he listed seven surprises for the 'Anglo-Saxons' as he put it. His analysis varied in its accuracy depending on which surprise or element was under consideration. Further, Kokoshin did not mention the biggest surprise of all to the coalition – that no weapons of mass destruction were found.

Kokoshin's first surprise was that the Anglo-Saxons no longer held an overwhelming supremacy in media coverage. CNN provided this superiority in the first conflict. Now, Kokoshin regarded Al-Jazeera as a political-psychological factor both in and beyond the Arab world. The US response to this charge would be that the US adapted to it by embedding Al-Jazeera into its web of reporters. An initial payback to the coalition occurred when the Arab world was able to watch Al-Jazeera's live coverage of the Iraqi joy and bedlam at the fall of the Hussein regime. This was a political-psychological step of the first order for the West. Kokoshin noted that the electronic media would eventually determine the moral and political winners and losers in this conflict.[18]

Second, Kokoshin noted that the US was surprised at the behavior of Turkey, considered one of America's most significant allies. The surprise was actually the failure of the Turkish General Staff to influence the Turkish government and parliament. Of course, Turkey recently had a change of government to a more fundamentalist point of view that influenced the situation greatly.

Third, Kokoshin noted that the US was surprised at the ferocity of the Shi'ite fighters in the south. On all three points, Kokoshin appears to have made good arguments.[19]

Fourth, Kokoshin noted that the inability of psychological operations troops to hasten the surrender of personnel and weapons on a scale similar to 1991 was a surprise.[20] US analysts would contend that Kokoshin was not aware of the different PSYOP goals this time around. The content of the leaflets and the situation had changed greatly since 1991. This required a new type of PSYOP. Iraq is not the desert of Kuwait, and Iraq's troops hadn't been subject to hours of B-52 bombs as they had been in 1991. Further, Iraqis fought for their land this time, which strengthened their will to resist. As expected, there were fewer prisoners of war. Further, most leaflets and PSYOP materials were not designed to cause surrender. In fact, the majority of the leaflets were designed to instruct Iraqis how to passively resist without sparking immediate regime retribution, and to warn Iraqis about the consequences of actions against coalition forces.

There were many examples that PSYOP did work. For example, one report indicated that the operators of an oilfield in southern Iraq primed the station to be blown, as Iraqi authorities there had directed. However, based on a leaflet warning operators about the consequences for Iraq's economy and future generations if the station was blown, the operators turned off the valves for the flow of oil. That is, the operators had satisfied the requirements of both parties! At the start of the conflict, Iraqis were instructed to go home instead of surrender, but this message was subtly changed as the operations wore on and the US continued to receive sniping in the rear area. Therefore Kokoshin's case for a 'surprise' in this case is not as strong. In fact, his analysis was unable to take into account all that was occurring.

Surprise five was that the US was unable to offset the system of state and military control in Iraq. CENTCOM would disagree, since most reports even in the first hours of the conflict indicated that Iraq's military command and control was disrupted. There was no large-scale resistance to the Third Infantry Division, and there appeared to be no coordinated mass and maneuver on the part of the Iraqis. General Vladimirov noted the same in his analysis above. Again, it must be remembered that this battlefield was not the Kuwaiti desert. Baghdad, the command and control center, was interconnected by a series of underground tunnels, and optical fiber had been laid in the past two years. Thus, the surprise might be that Iraqi command and control didn't last longer![21]

Surprise six to Kokoshin was the high efficiency of semi-armed formations. Many would agree with Kokoshin, as the Iraqis appeared to do well with harassing and guerrilla actions in the rear of US forces. It is hard to target small arms in the possession of thousands of people wearing civilian clothing, as US forces are finding out daily in their efforts to stabilize Iraq.[22]

Finally, Kokoshin noted that Saddam Hussein had changed from a tyrant to a hero in the Arab and Muslim world, one who didn't break under the might of the US military machine. Again the film of people bringing down Hussein's statues and tearing up his pictures would indicate that the Arab and Muslim world had seen another reaction to Hussein's rule.[23] Today, many people in Iraq fear that Hussein is still alive and might make a comeback. The Shia population is happy that Hussein has been deposed, so the Arab and Muslim world may be drawing a different conclusion from the one noted by Kokoshin. At a minimum, the feeling that Hussein is a hero is not universal among Arabs and Muslims.

Kokoshin, like most analysts worldwide, also incorrectly assessed how successful the US would be if it fought in Baghdad and how long it would take to capture the city. Few analysts, if any, were able to predict that Baghdad would be taken so quickly. One of Russia's preeminent military theorists, for example, General of the Army Makhmut Gareyev, also predicted a long siege of Baghdad, and expected the US to disrupt the life support system of the city and issue an ultimatum to the population. As Gareyev noted, many Russian experts had been mistaken in their predictions as to how the coalition would act, and he fell prey to the same problem.[24]

Finally, Kokoshin predicted that by storming the capital coalition forces would lose their ability to detect and hit an enemy at a larger distance. He also noted that only Israel had spent enough time on urban operations over the past few years. As anyone familiar with US theory would add, this was simply not true. The RAND corporation has published an entire series of documents about urban operations, the Pentagon stood up an urban operations task force a few years ago and the US studied intensely the numerous battles for Grozny (which Kokoshin recommended they do!) and trained fastidiously in urban operations at both JRTC and the National Training

Center (NTC). Kokoshin finished his article by noting that the US will achieve victory but not without huge losses and not as soon as many expected.[25]

In May Kokoshin expressed his concern that the war had heightened the degree of strategic indeterminacy in the world, as it had provoked the further proliferation of nuclear weapons and other forms of weapons of mass destruction and delivery systems, particularly in sensitive regions of the world. Kokoshin believes that for Russia this will mean improving its system for managing strategic nuclear forces, and reinforcing nuclear containment with pre-nuclear containment opportunities (use of high-precision, long-range weaponry with conventional, non-nuclear equipment against a defined class of military facilities and economic infrastructure objects).[26]

In regard to the regional issue, Kokoshin pointed to the increased likelihood that North Korea and Iran both see advantages in acquiring nuclear weapons. In particular North Korea's close ties with Pakistan should worry Washington. Both regimes appear to look at US interference in their regions as directed at regime change and not non-proliferation as stated, according to Kokoshin. Ukraine has also indicated it wants to access highly enriched uranium, and one should not forget Al-Qaeda's desire to exploit the proliferation desires of these countries.[27]

Of course, Kokoshin wasn't the only civilian defense official to address the war in Iraq. Aleksey Arbatov, a well-known civilian Duma Defense Committee member and deputy head of the committee, offered several incisive comments on the war and its impact on military reform in Russia. Arbatov's comments varied drastically from those of General Andrey Nikolayev, the committee's chairman. Instead of criticizing the West, Arbatov criticized the Russian military for both its lack of progress in military reform and for the logic it uses to view developments in the West.

Arbatov noted that the US surprised many strategic analysts with their ability to once again take few casualties and to limit collateral damage. But he also pointed out the lessons for military reform for Russia. He stressed the ability of the US professional (volunteer-contract) army to use the latest military equipment, something Arbatov believes a conscript force cannot do. As he summarized:

Who fights better, a soldier who has voluntarily arrived for military service and who receives a monetary reward from a grateful state for his professional labor and risk or a conscript who has been driven into the army by force, who doesn't know how to 'evade' and who does not desire to either serve or fight?... Soviet and Russian soldiers and officers' 'mass heroism and self-sacrifice' have too often atoned for the command authorities' lack of talent, the Army's lack of preparation, and the political leadership's irresponsibility.[28]

Further, Arbatov stated that the Ministry of Defense must now choose between quantity and quality. Quantity is currently at the center of Russian military policy and its force development. For this reason the army's maintenance budget line overwhelms the budget line for training and the development of new arms and equipment. Quality is important. A modern air force, as the Iraqi war demonstrated, is a vital commodity because even a limited number of high tech aircraft can support a ground force. In this sense, Arbatov does not recommend imitating the US but just following its example. He also supported the continued development in Russia of ground-based mobile missile systems that were so hard to find in Iraq.[29]

Finally Arbatov stated that Russian military specialists too often focus on only one aspect of a budgetary problem. For example, he noted how often Russian military leaders cite the amount of money allocated in the US budget to the military. What those same leaders do not like to cite is that this money is under the strict oversight of the Congress. Appropriations for defense are made public, which also causes a 'hypercritical examination for cost-effectiveness, for the conformity of new technology to operational-tactical concepts, and for the adequacy to actual, and not farfetched, security interests'.[30] Arbatov concluded his article by noting that this system of working in secrecy in Russia for the last 40 years has resulted in the majority of Russian defense troubles, including 'the growing technical lag' caused by the archaic decision-making system of the past.[31]

A few weeks later, Arbatov strongly criticized the West for its handling of the situation in Iraq after the war ended. He noted that the US lost its moral high ground and political leadership in the world, as well as the sympathy and support in Western Europe. The US wasted an immense amount of moral and political capital due to 'an intellectually inferior political leadership affected by tunnel vision'.[32] As such, a lesson learned was that 'a well-trained army can sometimes make up for the lack of foresight, statesmanship, and responsibility on the part of the political leadership'.[33]

SERVING OFFICERS

Some serving officers had little of value to add in the way of lessons learned. Russian air force commanders meeting in the Moscow region on 10 April, after the fight for Baghdad had ended noted that the US did nothing surprisingly new. The success of the effort was, after all, assured by the air force, the commanders added. Commander in Chief of the Air Force, Colonel General Vladimir Mikhaylov, stated the following:

We've analyzed what kinds of ammunition they used and how many sorties they performed. I would say that the number of sorties was excessive, as compared with the situation and the needs of ground troops. Sometimes the Americans were making mistakes and targeting their own troops. To put it briefly, we've thoroughly analyzed all their work.[34]

General of the Army Andrey Nikolayev, the chairman of the State Duma Defense Committee and Arbatov's boss on the committee, was more caustic in his remarks about the lessons of the war. On 24 April, in an interview with *Pravda*, he noted that US military strength is not accelerating the resolution of political problems, but creating new ones. The US specializes in bombing, detonating, killing and demolishing while leaving 'restoring' to others. The purpose of war for the US is to upgrade its warfare equipment, and the absence of a worthy adversary is creating conditions for the military recklessness of US political forces. Further, he noted that no credible opposition was presented against the US forces in Iraq (no enemy air force, navy, etc.) and that for ten years before the war, the US weakened Iraq economically, politically and militarily.

This, Nikolayev posited, was perhaps the main lesson that the US has taught the world – how to first prepare and then conduct war. Public opinion must be swayed first, then 'sins' of the regime developed, bans and sanctions announced, probing actions taken and potential allies gathered. Only then does military action proceed. A second essential lesson to learn is that the speed of development of military-political situations is outpacing the ability of Russia to create a modern military organization to keep up with the change. Military reform to date has only been to the advantage of those wishing to destroy Russia. Today, military reform that consolidates and doesn't destroy is needed, as well as a clear idea of the current military-political situation and the nature and essence of the state being defended.[35]

Current Chief of the General Staff Anatoliy Kvashnin was more specific in his comments. Kvashnin, in a 13 May interview, offered the opinion that both coalition troops and the Iraqi armed forces sustained tangible losses, the latter some three to five times higher. More interesting, Kvashnin discussed the fact that a 'system-level operation (*sistemnaya operatsiya*) was carried out in Iraq, which involved firepower, information and psychological pressure'. Coalition forces continued to develop their non-contact war model while also using more traditional weapons as well. Kvashnin cited as Iraqi mistakes the inability to construct necessary fortifications on the ground and the loss of control by the leadership over forces in Baghdad at a crucial time.[36] For Kvashnin the main conclusion of the war was that Russia needed to build its own armed forces on the basis of the plan approved by President Putin in 2001.

SERVING OFFICERS WRITE IN PROFESSIONAL JOURNALS: SOME NEGATIVE OBSERVATIONS

The May issue of the Russian military journal *Armeyskiy Sbornik* discussed lessons and conclusions from the blitzkrieg in Iraq. None of the lessons were complimentary toward the coalition and, in fact, even a neutral observer would conclude that some of the author's conclusions were absurd ('the Iraqis acted competently and decisively, the slightest bit of dust disabled an Abrams tank [did he not watch the duststorm?]', etc.). The author, Colonel Sergey Batyushkin, listed eight coalition mistakes and several Iraqi successes. The mistakes were:

- Political and diplomatic-level mistakes, such as the nuances of the geopolitical stance of Turkey. US officials ignored the Kurdish factor, according to Batyushkin.
- Forecasts of a walk in the park did not pan out. US forces were unable to achieve a quick victory. The impression of an Anglo-American army that was well-organized and streamlined evaporated after the first battles.
- US intelligence agencies did not provide accurate information to the military-political leadership. Coalition aircraft were unable to destroy engineering lines, communications lines, radar and air defense assets.

- Iraqi resistance was underestimated, and they forced their own tactical rules on the coalition. Forty per cent of coalition armored vehicle losses were from artillery fire, and the slightest amount of dust disabled coalition tanks according to Batyushkin.
- There were an insufficient number of allied troops for the operation.
- Excessive hopes were placed on technological superiority, especially on high-precision weapons. Troops equipped with such technology often lost tactically to the poorly-armed adversary who acted competently and decisively on the battlefield.
- Non-combat losses were almost equal to combat losses. There was a lack of coordination among coalition troops, and an excessive reliance on electronics.
- Insufficient attention was paid to maintaining the combat morale of the troops, logistical support and the everyday lives of the servicemen. The scarcity of tobacco reduced the low morale of the coalition servicemen even further.[37]

Batyushkin concluded by noting that the war showed how a poorly-armed adversary can put up stiff resistance, and how camouflage can spare troops from missiles and bomb strikes for a long time. It became clear that air defense is a very important asset in modern war to the Russians based on these and other comments. Batyushkin also concluded that the 'arrogant' Pentagon leaders underestimated the role of the human factor on the field of battle; that America cannot act alone, but needs allies; that aggression is perceived by the local population as an act of violence; and that other nations (North Korea, Iran, Syria) are already being measured for the prison robes of freedom and democracy American-style.[38] Batyushkin did not have a single good thing to say about the coalition's war effort, and it is difficult to consider him a scholar who can see both sides of a coin if this article is representative of his thinking.

A second article in *Armeyskiy Sbornik* was hardly critical at all of coalition efforts and in fact did nothing but describe coalition command and control mechanisms during the war. There was no analysis one way or the other as to the good and bad characteristics of the use of these systems. In conclusion, the authors, a Russian colonel and major-general, stated only that there were no clear victors in the war, and that even under near ideal conditions, systems still malfunctioned. Such systems need a separate and detailed analysis, according to the authors.[39]

In June, the Scientific Council of the Academy of Military Science held a session at which it discussed lessons learned from Iraq. Three long articles on the conference were published in *Red Star*, and a more detailed write-up of the conference was in the July issue of *Military Thought* (not covered in this analysis due to its length, and because this is the first of several installments). This indicates that many more articles are almost sure to appear.

The first of three articles in *Red Star* offered the thinking of both past and present officers on a variety of subjects. Colonel Aleksandr Korabelnikov discussed tactical lessons. He was impressed with how the coalition avoided head-on clashes by destroying the enemy first with combat aviation or helicopters; the effectiveness of intelligence units that allowed even company battalion-level commanders to receive systematized information; and the logistical ability of the coalition to keep replacements down by the timely supply of support to units. Korobelnikov correctly concluded that the real deciding factor in why the coalition achieved their objectives so fast was the lack of any Iraqi aviation, allowing coalition forces a free sky in which to fly. He also added that a permanent global war, with one superpower against the entire world, is being waged by all possible means (political, economic, information and military), and that America is transitioning to a system for deploying permanent mobilization forces, ready to strike without having to be deployed at any moment.[40]

Lieutenant-General Vladimir Barvinenko focused on the important role played by information operations. He noted that superiority was achieved not so much by the quantity and quality of aerial attack weaponry as by the complete information superiority of the coalition and its effective command and control. He cited achievements in information support and systems of rear and technical support. The creation of a joint information-command and control structure has created an information support system built on the functional integration of space-, air-, sea- and land-based information systems (reconnaissance, electronic warfare, communication, navigation, weapon guidance, automated processing, modeling, etc.) according to Barvinenko. These systems rely on the services of global telecommunication networks, both military and civilian. This allows the US to systematically observe a situation anywhere in the world, assess it and aim strike weapons there with precision if necessary. The main lesson for Russia from this war is that it also needs the ability to conduct joint operations utilizing all of these resources (especially air operations), according to Barvinenko.[41]

Other speakers at the session offered their assessments. Colonel-General Anatoliy Nogovitsin was impressed not only with precision weaponry but also with the effectiveness of electronic warfare and electronic intelligence. Major General Valeriy Menshikov added that the creation of a space infrastructure (reconnaissance, navigation, command, control, communications and relay systems) supporting space-based strike resources is a necessity. Since space-based navigation systems played such an important role in this war (the share of Navstar guided weapons was 95 per cent compared with seven per cent in 1991, Menshikov added), it is necessary for Russia to get its orbital groupings of satellites up to the required level.[42]

The second of the three articles in *Red Star* offered a somewhat more conservative view of the war. The authors included retired Major General Victor Ryabchuk, retired Lieutenant General Vasiliy Reznichenko, Major General Valeriy Cheban, Colonel Anatoliy Tsyganok and General of the Army Andrey Nikolayev, the conservative chairman of the State Duma Committee on Defense.

Colonel Tsyganok noted that the war had two phases. The first phase was an active defense by two Iraqi Army corps around Basra, al-Najir, al-Nasiriyah and other cities. The second stage was the so-called 'strange defense of Baghdad'. Tsyganok believed that the coalition took more losses than were reported, that the sand storm consumed equipment and disabled over 100 armored vehicles, thermal imaging devices malfunctioned on over 150 vehicles, and the identification friend or foe system between aircraft and armored vehicles didn't work. Finally, citing Arab reports, Tsyganok stated that the US bribed three Iraqi generals, and over a year ago had concluded a deal that the Republican Guard forces would not participate in engagements. Again, Tsyganok believed the foreign press but not the US press, and formed his opinions based on these sources.[43]

Retired Major General Ryabchuk, a specialist on systemology, commented briefly on the US information-propaganda support plan, which was used to seize the initiative, and then focused on the US use of information-technical equipment. He wrongly stated that over 70 per cent of precision-guided munitions flew off into the desert. He more correctly determined that decoy targets and radar masking systems were used to some effect by the Iraqis. He concluded by stating that:

I think the experience of this war has once again confirmed the priority of Russia's military science in the development of battlefield command and control theory and the transformation of information rivalry into an intellectual-information rivalry. Sun Tsu's postulate that 'he fights well who controls the enemy and does not permit the enemy to control him' is well developed in our country in military systemology and battlefield and operations command and control theory as single systemic processes... it raises the question that the times of independent operations of the branches and types of troops are receding into the past and that the problem of the command and control of joint operations of inter-branch groupings under single leadership based upon a single concept of operations and planning is becoming the priority.[44]

Ryabchuk concluded by stating that the US competently used a combination of two things: an intellectual-information-navigation-reconnaissance system and an information-psychological aggression plan.[45]

Retired Lieutenant General Reznichenko discussed the series of computer-simulated war games that the US regularly runs with regard to the Caspian region. He cited a TRADOC spokesman (unnamed) as having stated that the Caspian region is the area and theater of war serving as the criterion for reform of the US ground forces as a result of the new geopolitical situation. There were two reasons for citing this comment. First, he was warning the Russian hierarchy that this might be one of the next regions in the Pentagon's sights and, second, he wanted the General Staff to be aware that talk of the uselessness of ground forces and only non-contact war, as advocated by a few retired Russian generals, was nonsense. In particular, he noted that the Russian North Caucasus Military District should prepare forces that are capable of combating US plans for the latter's 'future forces'. Reznichenko also proposed that the Russian president should try to ban precision-guided systems in a speech at the United Nations.[46]

Major General Cheban discussed some of the ideological and psychological components of the US plan. In particular he noted that the US spreads its ideology throughout the world before a conflict begins in order to propagandize the justice and sanctity of US military policy, and to point out the defects of dictatorial regimes. At the same time this policy, in Cheban's opinion, hid Iraqi successes and increased enemy losses while hiding information on friendly fire losses.[47]

Finally, General of the Army Nikolayev stated his opinion on the war. He viewed the war as less than a full-scale test since there was no organized military resistance, no opposition to the US navy or air force. He felt that the main lesson of the war to be the demonstration of the technology of preparation and conduct of modern war conducted as if on a test range. If a country's economic and military potential and morale fall, then the US is ready to step in and threaten its security. Any country is capable of becoming a test range. Nikolayev noted that these test ranges are 'located without fail in direct proximity to reserves of oil, gas, and bioresources, and have natural and production values, in short, those things that pose an interest for the US's missionary path...'.[48]

The President of the Academy of Military Sciences, General of the Army Makhmut Gareyev, authored the final article of the series. Gareyev's discussion, as usual, was full of important points as well as criticism of the coalition effort.

Gareyev opened his article on the offensive, discussing the military-political impact of the operation. He stated that the goal of the operation was not to find weapons of mass destruction but to obtain oil and to resolve economic problems which thereby would strengthen the US's geopolitical position. He stated that the 'last rites' were bestowed on the multipolar world as a result, that a sort of capitalist colonial ideology is being thrown on the world, and that the operation violated international law, the principle of the inviolability of state sovereignty. The entire operation, Gareyev stated, is buttressed by a US campaign of an information nature to vindicate and justify its expansionist policy. This opinion coincides in many ways with the opinion of Nikolayev.[49]

Gareyev underscored how US policy ascertained that countries must toe the line in response to US desires. For example, he cited how the US limits it trade with Russia, opposes Georgian and Azerbaijani cooperation with Russia in the oil and gas sphere and supports the movement of NATO troops to Russia's border. At the same time, he added, the US financed and armed the Taliban against Russia, and helped Saddam Hussein in the war against Iran. Gareyev noted, 'If we are going to nourish terrorism at the state level and then fight it, the fight will go on forever'.[50]

Gareyev, however, underscored that fact that in spite of these contradictions in US policy, there is still a vital need for the US and Russia to cooperate on the important issues at the end of the day. These include the issues of security, energy resources, terrorism and the proliferation of weapons of mass destruction. He added, 'There is no better way to spite a friend than to always agree with him'. Thus, he believes it is out of respect for America itself than Russia must speak out without constraint against what it considers adventurism in politics.[51]

As regards the US plan for the operation, Gareyev noted that the US command relied on 'subversive actions, bribery and treason of the highest political and military leaders of Iraq, as the most effective type of precision weapon'.[52] Gareyev clearly believed that the US had conducted secret negotiations with members of the Presidential Guard before the war started in order to avert a prolonged and destructive fight, and that many in the Iraqi military leadership accepted payments for their noninvolvement in the operation.

Gareyev felt the coalition did a great job of reconnaissance before the war started, both from internal agents and from space reconnaissance assets. He also mentioned that reconnaissance helicopters, the E8 JSTARS, and E-3 AWACS, along with tactical radar reconnaissance aircraft and stations, operated well. Aviation was linked to a system of reconnaissance-strike complexes. Night vision instruments and navigational hardware ensured reliable ground operations. Gareyev contended that the man in the link is still the only item that cannot be replaced, since space components still can be neutralized by use of appropriate interference assets.[53]

When listing US and British casualties, Gareyev listed both figures from US and foreign sources. That is, his analysis appeared to be much more balanced than that of some of his cohorts at the conference. On the other hand, he accused the coalition of deliberately bombing markets, hospitals, hotels and other installations in order to terrify the populace and troops in order to compel capitulation.[54]

Gareyev offered five conclusions in his article.

First, like Nikolayev, he underscored the political-diplomatic, economic, information, psychological and military preparation of a country in order to turn it into a rogue state, ready for intervention with public support.

Second, Gareyev did not see any serious developments in military art, since this was not a war with a strong adversary, noting that the war was as much a unilateral exercise as a war (which anyone who fought there would violently disagree with!). Gareyev did state that the organizational structure of the US forces, lacking a regimental level, did not justify itself, but he offered no reason as to why. Interestingly, he added, 'statements by some of our critics that the Iraq war dispelled the myth about the precision weapon and the high-tech war, about the professionalism of the American Army, and certain others, appear out of keeping with what actually occurred'. Gareyev believes that US equipment is the strongest feature of the US Army, providing a sense of helplessness and doom to the enemy's will to resist.

Third, he stated that conclusions of so-called experts of the forecasts of future war were not justified. In this sense, Gareyev sensed the greater degree of flexibility in US operations than others apparently sensed. The basics (operation, battle, regrouping, etc.) have not changed, he believed – just the conditions, forms and methods of their implementation. Thus he understood perhaps better than other analysts that not every war has to start with an extended air campaign, but on the conditions and situation at hand.

Fourth, it is clear that the substance of reform of the Russian armed forces must not only be to adapt to terrorism, but also to fulfill defensive tasks. There are many other threats to Russia, for which it needs diverse and powerful regular troops.

Finally, Gareyev believes the US armed forces did not defeat the Russian military system, which Hussein adopted. It is not necessary to adopt the US system as a result. Gareyev asked 'which of the Soviet or Russian tenets of military science and military art did not survive the tests of the Iraqi war?'[55]

CONCLUSIONS

The war in Iraq did result in several important discoveries and lessons learned, according to Russian specialists. In many cases they were not the lessons that the West expected Russia would learn. One specialist decided that the US prepares for an intervention some ten years in advance, preparing the way with an extended economic and psychological operation. Another stated that a new armed forces for Russia must be formed, one with a new 'genetic code'. Yet another specialist wrote that the real lessons lie in the unintended consequence of motivating the further proliferation of nuclear weapons, and in the formation of a new system of international relations. Soviet-minded specialists tended to discount US press accounts and relied more heavily on foreign (even Arab) accounts of the fighting to draw their conclusions regarding casualties, successes and defeats, and so on.

Russian officers seldom mentioned the dissolution of several myths about the US armed forces in their lessons learned. Before the war, these were prominent issues in the press – for example, that coalition forces weren't willing to take casualties, and that US forces always have nuclear weapons at the trigger-ready position. Most important, not a single Russian analyst noted that one should not 'template coalition forces' as many of Russia's top experts attempted to do before the war. Only 80-year-old General of the Army Gareyev stated that conditions, forms and methods would change, but tactics and strategy would not. Thus, Gareyev did not discount coalition flexibility in their application of war plans. Other Russian analysts appeared to rely more on recognized trends from past operations than any creative attempt to predict the form of current operations.

Perhaps the reason for this oversight was that it appeared to be a simple task to predict what course of action coalition forces would take in Iraq. The examples of Kosovo and 'Desert Storm' certainly indicated that a massive air assault would be followed by a quick peace or perhaps the use of ground forces to conduct a peacekeeping action. However, the course of action settled on at CENTCOM and the adaptations they made along the way (operational pause, reaction to attacks in the rear, etc.) came as a surprise not only to US analysts but also to Russian specialists. The surprise was not limited just to the manner in which the war was conducted (more reliance on ground forces than originally thought) but also with regard to the speed of action and the ease with which objectives were taken. For example, it would be difficult to find any analyst worldwide who might have projected a simple drive into Baghdad to secure and take it.

Russian analysts should heed Gareyev's advice and consider in greater detail potential courses of action in future conflicts. This war showed that templating coalition actions wouldn't work. But the analysis of the operation by Russian military specialists highlighted many other lessons that the Russian military took from the conflict. Among many, these included the development of a systems-level operation by US forces (firepower, information, psychological) and – according to several military analysts – the implication that Russian military reform must not linger any longer nor fail to be affected by what has happened in Iraq. The lingering question is: how many of the important and influential military voices believe in true military reform and want to see it implemented?

Throwing off the final vestiges of the old military system (cadres, armaments, etc.) will be difficult. However, Russian military science, superior in many ways to that of any other country in the world, will not change and will always keep Russia potentially strong.

NOTES

The views expressed in this report are those of the author and do not necessarily represent the official policy or position of the Department of the Army, Department of Defense, or the US government.

The Foreign Military Studies Office (FMSO) assesses regional military and security issues through open-source media and direct engagement with foreign military and security specialists to advise army leadership on issues of policy and planning critical to the US Army and the wider military community.

1. Igor Rodionov, 'Reform will Destroy our Army', RosBusinessConsulting, 24 July 2003, article received by email from William O'Malley on 26 July 2003.
2. Vitaliy Denisov, 'Increasing the Effectiveness of the Militarized Bloc', *Red Star*, 30 July 2003, as translated and downloaded from the FBIS website on 30 July 2003.
3. Moscow Channel One TV, 1930 GMT, 1 April 2003, as translated and downloaded from the FBIS website on 1 April 2003.
4. Leonid Shershnev, 'With a Major Plan', *Vremya Novostey*, 9 April 2003, as translated and downloaded from the FBIS website on 9 April 2003.
5. Ibid.
6. Ilya Kriger, 'Equating Saddle to Tank', *Novaya Gazeta*, html version, 17 April 2003 as translated and downloaded from the FBIS website on 17 April 2003.
7. Ibid.
8. Vladimir Slipchenko, 'Incontinent Power. Even the Possible Deaths of Half a Million Iraqis Cannot Stop the Flywheel of War', *Rossiyskaya Gazeta*, 22 Feb. 2003, as translated and downloaded from the FBIS website on 25 Feb. 2003.
9. V.G. Reznichenko, 'Determining the Character of the Armed Forces', *Voyennaya Mysl*, 14 April 2003, as translated and downloaded from the FBIS website on 5 May 2003.
10. Vladimir Slipchenko, 'Syria Had Better be Afraid', *Rossiyskaya Gazeta*, 3 April 2003, as translated and downloaded from the FBIS website on 3 April 2003.
11. Interview with Vladimir Slipchenko, *Kommercant' Vlact'*, 28 April–4 May 2003, p.39.
12. Interview with Aleksandr Vladimirov, Moscow Informatsionnoye Agentstvo Ekho Moskvy, 1103 GMT, 2 May 2003, as translated and downloaded from the FBIS website on 2 May 2003.
13. Interview with Aleksandr Vladimirov by Maksim Kalashnikov, 'A Baghdad Quiz for Russia', *Russkiy Predprinimatel*, 15 June 2003, as translated and downloaded from the FBIS website on 15 June 2003.
14. Ibid.

15. Vladimir Dvorkin, 'Urgent and Immediate Matters. On Some Preliminary Lessons of the War in Iraq', *Nezavisimaya Gazeta*, 4 April 2003, p.9, as translated and downloaded from the FBIS website on 7 April 2003.
16. Andrei Lebedev, 'If You Want Peace, Prepare for the Right Kind of War', *Izvestia*, 7 May 2003, p.3 as reported in *The Current Digest* 55/20 (2003) pp.7, 8.
17. Leonid Ivashov, 'War in Iraq: Unequal Struggle of Weapon Systems', *Military Parade*, May/June 2003, pp. 88, 89.
18. Andrei Kokoshin, 'Seven Surprises from the War in Iraq', *Nezavisimaya Gazeta*, 7 April 2003.
19. Ibid.
20. Ibid.
21. Ibid.
22. Ibid.
23. Ibid.
24. Moscow, *Agentstvo Voyennykh Novostey*, 0907 GMT, 4 April 2003, as translated and downloaded from the FBIS website on 4 April 2003.
25. Kokoshin.
26. Interview with Andrey Kokoshin, 'The Iraq War is Provoking the Proliferation of Nuclear Weapons', *Politbyuro* (Internet Version-WWW), 12 May 2003, as translated and downloaded from the FBIS website on 12 May 2003.
27. Andrei Kokoshin, 'Russia's Role in Non-Proliferation: Obstacles and Opportunities', *In the National Interest*, 7 May 2003, from website <http://www. inthenationalinterest.com>.
28. Aleksey Arbatov, 'Military Reform in Light of Other People's Error's: The Decision Making System in the Russian Army Lags Behind by Several Generations', *Nezavisimoye Voyennoye Obozreniye*, 23 May 2003, as translated and downloaded from the FBIS website on 23 May 20003.
29. Ibid.
30. Ibid.
31. Ibid.
32. Aleksey Arbatov, 'Iraq Lessons', *Moscow News*, 18–24 June 2003, email from William O'Malley.
33. Ibid.
34. Moscow TVS, 1100 GMT, 10 April 2003, as translated and downloaded from the FBIS website on 14 April 2003.
35. Andrey Nikolayev, 'Fundamental Lessons of the War in Iraq', *Pravda*, 24 April 2003, as translated and downloaded from the FBIS website on 24 April 2003.
36. Moscow RIA-Novosti, 1442 GMT, 13 May 2003, as translated and downloaded from the FBIS website on 13 May 2003.
37. Sergey Batyushkin, 'Just a Few Mistakes...', *Armeyskiy Sbornik*, 1 May 2003, as translated and downloaded from the FBIS website on 1 May.
38. Ibid.
39. Vladimir Chernykh and Yevgeniy Kozlov, 'Shock and Awe – No Clear Victor?' *Armeyskiy Sbornik*, 31 May 2003, as translated and downloaded from the FBIS website on 31 May.
40. Oleg Falichev, 'Secret Springs of the War in Iraq', *Krasnaya Zvezda*, 28 June 2003, as translated and downloaded from the FBIS website on 28 June 2003.

41. Ibid.
42. Ibid.
43. Oleg Falichev, 'Secret Springs of the War in Iraq', *Red Star*, 8 July 2003, as translated and downloaded from the FBIS website on 8 July 2003, report of the Russian Academy of Military Sciences on lessons of Iraq war.
44. Ibid.
45. Ibid.
46. Ibid.
47. Ibid.
48. Ibid.
49. Makhmut Gareyev, 'Silent Springs of the Iraq War', *Red Star*, 18 July 2003, p.2.
50. Ibid.
51. Ibid.
52. Ibid.
53. Ibid.
54. Ibid.
55. Ibid.

About the Contributors

Mikhail Tsypkin is an Associate Professor of national security at the Naval Postgraduate School in Monterey, CA, USA.

Alexander A. Belkin is Deputy Executive Director of the Council on Foreign and Defense Policy, Moscow.

Alexander Golts is a Deputy Editor-In-Chief of the Russian Weekly, *Yezhenedelny Zhurnal*, and an observer of military affairs.

Richard Giragosian is a Washington-based analyst specializing in international relations and military security in the former Soviet Union, the Middle East and Asia-Pacific region. He is a former Professional Staff Member of the U.S. Senate and is a regular contributor to the publications of Radio Free Europe/Radio Liberty and Jane's Information Group, among other publications.

Mikhail Pogorely is Director of the Center for War and Peace Journalism, Moscow.

Alexander G. Savelyev is a Researcher at the Institute of World Economy and International Relations (IMEMO) in Moscow.

Vitaly Shlykov is advisor to the General Director of the United Heavy Machinery (Uralmash-Izhora Group) Company, Moscow.

Lester W. Grau is a military analyst with the Foreign Military Studies Office, For Leavenworth, KS, USA.

Timothy L. Thomas is an analyst at the Foreign Military Studies Office (FMSO) at Fort Leavenworth, Kansas. He retired from the U.S. Army as a Lieutenant Colonel in the summer of 1993. Mr. Thomas received a B.S. from West Point and an M.A. from the University of

Southern California. He was a U.S. Army Foreign Area Officer who specialized in Soviet/Russian studies. His military assignments included serving as the Director of Soviet Studies at the United States Army Russian Institute (USARI) in Garmisch, Germany; as an inspector of Soviet tactical operations under CSCE; and as a Brigade S-2 and company commander in the 82nd Abn Division. Mr. Thomas has done extensive research and publishing in the areas of peacekeeping, information war, psychological operations, low intensity conflict, and political-military affairs. He is the assistant editor of the journal European Security; an adjunct professor at the U.S. Army's Eurasian Institute; an adjunct lecturer at the USAF Special Operations School; and a member of two Russian organizations, the Academy of International Information, and the Academy of Natural Sciences.

INDEX

For Product Safety Concerns and Information please contact our EU
representative GPSR@taylorandfrancis.com
Taylor & Francis Verlag GmbH, Kaufingerstraße 24, 80331 München, Germany